Introduction to **Indian Architecture**

text by Bindia Thapar
illustrations by Suparna Bhalla and Surat Kumar Manto

PERIPLUS

Published by Periplus Editions with editorial offices at
130 Joo Seng Road #06-01, Singapore 368357

Text copyright © 2004 Bindia Thapar
Illustrations © 2004 Suparna Bhalla and Surat Kumar Manto

ISBN 0-7946-0011-5

Distributors
North America, Latin America, and Europe: Tuttle Publishing,
364 Innovation Drive, North Clarendon, VT 05759-9436
tel: (802) 773 8930 ; fax: (802) 773 6993
e-mail: info@tuttlepublishing.com; www.tuttlepublishing.com

Asia Pacific: Berkeley Books Pte Ltd, 130 Joo Seng Road #06-01/03, Singapore
368357; tel (65) 6280 1330; fax (65) 6280 6290
e-mail: inquiries@periplus.com.sg; www.periplus.com

Japan: Tuttle Publishing, Yaekari Building, 3F, 5-4-12 Osaki,
Shinagawa-ku; Tokyo 141-0032; tel: (813) 5437 0171;
fax: (813) 5437 0755; e-mail: tuttle-sales@gol.com

Picture Credits
top (t); bottom (b); middle (m); left (l), right (r)

P. Aditya: pp. 23 (r, m, b), 26 (b), 78 (bl), 79, 140 (t); *Suparna Bhalla*: pp. 10 (ml),
11, 30, 31 (r), 33 (b), 34 (b), 37 (b), 42 (tl & m), 45 (t), 47 (r), 49 (r), 50 (l), 52 (t),
53 (tl), 58 (b), 60, 69 (b), 71 (t), 78 (b), 80 (b), 85 (r), 88 (t & b), 92 (t & br), 99,
107 (t), 109 (br), 114–15 (b), 115 (mr), 116 (b), 119 (b), 126 (ml), 127 (m), 132 (tl),
134 (b), 137 (b); *Michael Freeman*: endpapers, pp. 1, 2, 4–5, 6, 8–9, 38–9, 86–7,
90–1, 93, 120–1; *R. K. Gaur*: pp. 10 (b), 18–19 (t), 22, 25 (mr), 31 (t & b), 32 (t),
41 (br), 54 (b), 65 (b), 68 (b), 97 (tr), 105 (t), 108 (t), 109 (t), 112 (tl), 112–13 (b),
113, 118 (m); *Robert Harding*: pp. 40–1 (b); *Alpana Khare*: p. 19 (b); *Rupinder
Khullar*: pp. 14, 15 (t), 16 (t), 17 (tr), 21 (b), 23 (t), 32 (b), 34 (t), 37 (t), 40 (t), 41
(tr), 42 (br), 44 (b), 45 (r), 46, 48 (t), 49 (l), 51 (b), 55 (t), 56, 57 (b), 58 (t), 59 (br),
64 (t), 69 (t), 70 (b), 71 (b), 78 (ml), 80 (tl), 82, 83 (br), 85 (t), 92 (bl), 95, 96, 98
(tl), 99, 100 (tl & br), 101, 110–11, 116 (t), 118 (tl & b), 122 (t), 123 (tl), 133, 134
(t), 135, 136, 137 (t), 138, 139, 141 (t); *Surat Kumar Manto*: pp. 16 (b), 29 (t), 40
(bl), 52 (b), 55 (b), 77, 82–3, 94–5, 98, 102–3 (b), 112 (bl), 129 (t); *National Museum, New Delhi*: pp. 10 (tl), 28 (t), 29 (b), 84 (t); *V. Muthuraman*: pp. 13, 17 (tl
& br), 48 (b), 53 (tr & b), 57 (t & m), 59 (t), 125; *John Panikar*: p. 140 (b); *G. C.
Otto*: pp. 12 (ml), 36, 47 (b), 124 (lt & r); *Otto Pfister*: p. 25 (ml); *Ram Rehman*:
p. 141 (b); *Raj Rewal*: p. 142; *Kamal Sahai*: pp. 12 (br), 15 (b), 50 (br), 70 (t), 89,
123 (tr & b), 124 (bl), 127 (b), 130, 131; *Ayesha Sarkar*: p. 76 (t); *Toby Sinclair*:
pp. 28 (b), 132 (b); *B. B. S. Walia*: pp. 12 (tl), 19 (m), 21 (mr), 26 (t), 27, 35, 43,
44 (t), 47 (t), 54 (t), 61, 62 (t & br), 63, 65 (t & m), 68 (t), 76 (b), 78 (t), 81, 84 (b),
103, 104, 105 (b), 107 (b), 109 (bl), 114 (t l), 115 (t & ml), 116 (m), 117, 119 (tl
& r), 129 (b); *Henry Wilson*: pp. 3, 18, 20, 21 (tl & r), 24, 25 (tl & r), 33 (t), 51 (t),
62 (bl), 64 (b), 66, 67, 72, 73, 74, 75, 80 (ml), 88 (m), 97 (tl), 100 (ml), 106, 108
(b), 122 (b), 127 (t), 129.

Endpapers: Detail of the original blue, white and yellow tilework on the façade of the
Man Mandir palace at Gwalior Fort. **Page 1:** Two of the *gopurams* viewed across the
tank in the second enclosure of the Arunachaleshvara Temple in Tiruvannmalai. **Page
2:** The free-standing Diwan-i-Khas or Hall of Private Audience at the palace complex of
Fatehpur Sikri. **Page 3:** Muslim influence in the floral decoration on the pillar capitals
of a building. **This page:** The ornate screened façade of the Hawa Mahal in Jaipur
where women could sit in seclusion enjoying the view and the breezes. **Page 6:**
Rock-cut Jain statues below Gwalior Fort.

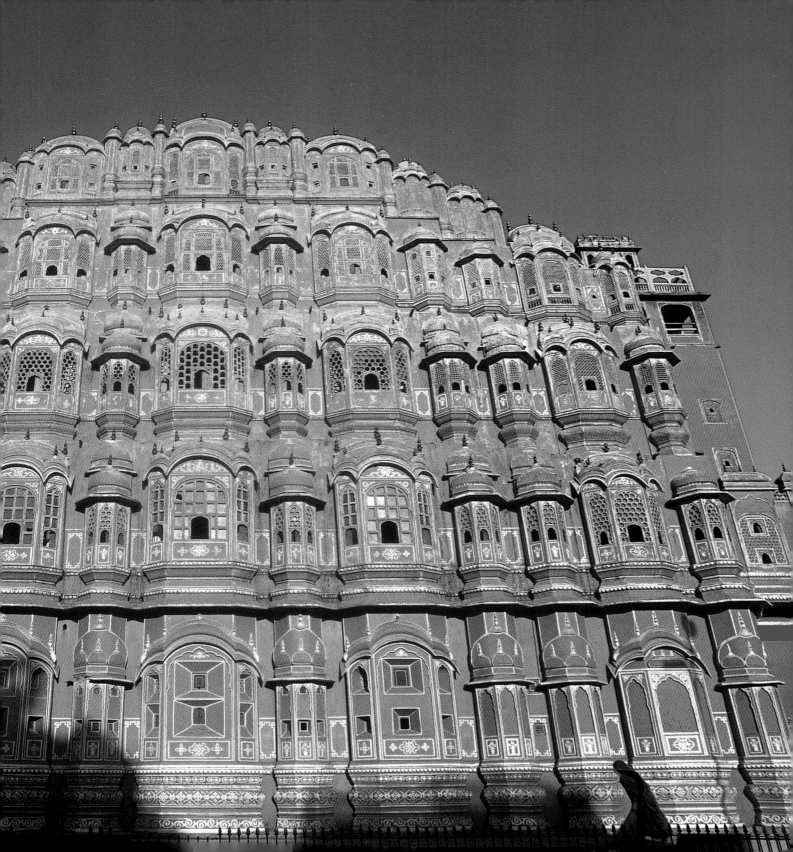

Contents

The ancient hill fort of Gwalior, gateway to central India, which stretches 3 kilometers across a 100-meter-high rocky plateau. Its long and eventful history led to an interesting amalgam of Hindu, Jain and Islamic architectural features. The fort encompasses a number of palaces, temples and tanks.

Introduction

The unique geography of India has contributed greatly to its historical and cultural developments. The Himalayas ring the north, while the river basins, desert wastelands and Deccan plateau cover much of the peninsula which is encircled by the Arabian Sea to the west, the Bay of Bengal to the east and the Indian Ocean to the south. Landscape, climate and history have all shaped the architecture of India.

One of the most notable of the small steatite seals discovered at Mohenjodaro is the image of the Indian humped bull with its pronounced muscularity and a heavy dewlap. Despite its diminutive size, it still conveys an impression of immense strength and power. Other animals commonly depicted on these seals include the elephant, the bison and the crocodile.

The Vedic (or fire) altar was the first formal place of worship, built more than 3,000 years ago of brick. It represented the cosmic worlds of celestial space, the terrestrial world and the world of air.

Among the earliest examples of Gupta architecture are the caves at Udaygiri (4th–5th century AD). They are primarily rock-cut cells of a primitive nature, carved into a sandstone hill near Bhopal in Madhya Pradesh.

The history of the country has its beginnings in the valley of the Indus River, where 5,000 years ago, around 3000 BC, a remarkable civilisation flourished. Whole cities have been excavated, and a range of artefacts found, but much of the civilisation still remains a mystery because its script has not yet been deciphered. However, the statuettes, seals and other implements found tell of an agrarian society which worshipped, amongst other things, the concept of fertility. This civilisation had trade and other links with contemporary civilisations of the west, contacts being maintained by caravans traveling through mountain passes of the Himalayas.

The Indus valley civilisation declined about 2000 BC. The causes are not known, but could include drought, floods or drying up of trade.

The Arrival of Hinduism

About 400 years later, various Central Asian tribes began crossing over into India. This migration of fair-skinned people, called the Indo-Aryans, who spoke a language deriving from the same source as Latin and Greek, is again shrouded in mystery for an entirely different set of reasons. The Indo-Aryans were pastoral. They worshipped fire and had anthropomorphic gods and well-established rituals of prayer which were coded in a set of oral texts called the *Vedas*, which only assumed a literary form 500 years later. Their religion eventually came to be known as Hinduism. The Aryans settled down in the fertile plain of the Ganges River, subjugated the native tribes, and started the process of cultural assimilation that has been one of the hallmarks of the Indian subcontinent's history. Unfortunately, even though literary texts provide us with some evidence of the architectural activities of the time, no archaeological evidence remains.

Aryan society was divided into four *varna* or castes, of which the uppermost, the *brahmanas*, monopolised Vedic religion. Reaction against this led to the birth of several dissident religions in the subcontinent, including Buddhism and Jainism. Buddhism was founded in

the 5th century BC, and received royal patronage 200 years later under the Mauryan king Ashoka, who converted to the faith after a bloody battle fought against the king of Kalinga (in Orissa) on the eastern coast of India. It was around this time that Alexander of Macedonia reached India, and though he eventually did not succeed in extending his empire to this part of the world, his invasion brought the tradition of stone carving to the Indian subcontinent. Ashoka used the knowledge of stone craft to begin the tradition of stone architecture in India, dedicated to Buddhism. Proof that prior to this period Indian architecture had a strong, well-developed tradition of building in wood, bamboo and thatch is available in the forms created in stone by Ashoka's architects and craftsmen. All the architecture of the period shows that wooden structural forms, especially those of column, beam and lintel, were being replicated in stone.

The Mauryas and the Guptas

The first great Indian empire was founded by Chandragupta Maurya in 321 BC and his capital at Pataliputra (Patna) is reputed to have been the largest city in the world at the time. A sound administrative system, clear-cut social order, peace and security established a firm foundation that led to the rule of Ashoka, a great and visionary emperor. Although he ruthlessly expanded his kingdom during the first eight years of his rule, Ashoka's conversion to Buddhism thereafter caused him to espouse non-violence while maintaining a pragmatism in all matters of governance. Only the most southernmost kingdoms of the peninsula remained independent while Ashoka's empire extended across the length and breadth of the rest of India. The extent of his kingdom is evident from the thousands of *stupas*, pillars and rocks bearing Buddhist edicts erected by Ashoka. His legacy lives on in the Sarnath pillar decorated with four lions that has been adopted as an emblem of independent India.

After the Mauryas, it was not until almost 500 years later that another great dynasty united the country and gave the creative arts and matters of governance inspired patronage.

During the era of the Guptas, also referred to as the Golden or Classical Age, the Hindu temple, in particular, acquired an ornate image with the embellishment of extravagant sculptures.

A contemporary map showing India's historical sites.

11

The Earliest Architectural Traditions

The earliest traditions of building in stone in the Indian subcontinent were those of cave and rock-cut architecture, inspired by itinerant Buddhist monks. Later, the caves excavated by these monks were cut into to create ornate interiors. Gradually, the transition from rock-cut to stone-made architecture took place all over the subcontinent, and the monumental architecture of this period, built to survive through time, is all stone-cut or stone-made.

Buddhist, Jain and Hindu architecture continued to be created all over the subcontinent, with a constant overlap and synthesis. St Thomas had reached the southern shores of India in AD 52, and some churches may have been built, but again no evidence remains, and the predominant monumental architectural activity in the subcontinent at this time was inspired by Buddhism, Jainism and Hinduism. The iconography of all three religions began to show a fair degree of synthesis of content and form, and many elements originating in one religious tradition were adopted by the others, once again demonstrating the inherent secularism within each diverse cultural tradition.

Although various Central Asian tribes, such as the Kushanas and the Shakas, continued to migrate into India, their religious and cultural identities had the space that the diversity of cultural traditions in India provided and they gradually got assimilated into the complex Indian social structure. Racially and linguistically, however, there were the two major groupings of northern Aryans and southern Dravidians, but there also existed many other indigenous tribes in the eastern, northeastern and central regions with their own distinct cultural identities.

Central and North Indian Kingdoms

Within the country, the first millennium AD was a period of several kingdoms, many of them petty, many with imperial ambitions, which were involved in an almost constant struggle for political supremacy.

Between about AD 750 and 900, there was a tripartite struggle for power between the Palas in Bihar and Bengal in the east, the Pratiharas, descendants of the Rajasthani Gurjaras of central India, and the Rashtrakutas of the Deccan. Constant conflict eventually depleted their resources, resulting in their decline.

Top: Gateway to the Sanchi *stupa*, one of the finest examples of early Buddhist architecture.

Above: The earliest tradition of building in stone was that of rock-cut architecture, as seen in the Ellora Caves.

Right: This finely carved terracotta panel is from Vishnupur, west Bengal. In the absence of stone, terracotta was widely used in the region for both the structural form (derived from the thatched hut) and for decoration.

In the south, the Cholas, still a minor kingdom at the tip of the peninsula, were to achieve political and cultural hegemony between AD 862 and 1310, with an embassy of Chola merchants reaching as far as China in AD 1077.

Architecturally, this period saw prolific building activity, particularly in the south, with religious architecture dominating and some of the most well-known architectural masterpieces of India built in this period, often by minor historical figures. In fact, it can be generally said that perhaps in no other art as much as in architecture did religion play such a pivotal role in forming stylistic identities and associations, enhanced by India's artistic energies to absorb varying influences.

Eastern Renaissance

In Kalinga, in modern-day Orissa (and further east in Bengal), there was a brief but vibrant spurt of building activity between AD 700 and 1250. A unique style of temple architecture flourished in Bhubaneshwar, the artistic and religious capital of the region, which eventually merged in the south with the Dravidian forms and spread its influence westward toward Rajasthan. Beyond Bhubaneshwar, Konarak and further east, the terracotta temples of Gaur and Vishnupur, Bengal, both add brief but glorious chapters to the history of Hindu architecture's development north of the Vindhya range.

The Advent of Islam

Between AD 1001 and 1025, Mahmud of Ghazni (a small town in Afghanistan) plundered India seventeen times. Later, in AD 1192, on the country's northern frontiers, Mohammad Ghauri, a Turkish warlord from the steppes of Central Asia, advanced deep into the region and overthrew the Rajput king Prithviraj Chauhan, marking the political entry of Islam in India. Islam itself had touched India in the 8th century AD through Sind on the western shores, but it was only in the 12th century AD that a dynasty was established that had a different religious identity to the prevailing faith. The Mamluk or Slave dynasty was the first of the Muslim dynasties to be established in India, where it maintained its strong identity of culture and religion.

The Muslims introduced a new structural system, the arcuate system of construction, with its arch and dome, into the existing architectural vocabulary based on the trabeate system of beam, column and lintel. They also introduced

The Parsvanatha Temple is one of the most magnificent of the temples of Khajuraho (11th century AD).

The Jama Masjid in Delhi is the largest mosque in India. It was built by the Mughal emperor Shah Jahan in 1656 and took six years to complete. The 28-meter-square courtyard accommodates up to 20,000 people at prayer time. The central arch is framed by two minarets, behind which three black and white marble domes cover the prayer hall inside.

a new form of decoration, based on geometry and calligraphy, into the already present iconographic imagery of Hinduism, Buddhism and Jainism. Over the next 700 years, art, architecture, music and literature saw a synthesis of traditions from all these religions, and the creation of a distinct style of aesthetics.

Even though it was in Delhi that Islam had established its Indian empire, the rest of India, including the Deccan, soon saw smaller provincial governments emerging. The uneasy truce between these Islamic kingdoms and the established Hindu kingdoms was broken occasionally. Architecturally, however, the cross influence of both cultures proved to be both invigorating as well as long-lasting.

The Great Mughals

In AD 1526, Babur, a young prince from Samarkand in Central Asia, defeated the Delhi sultan Ibrahim Lodi, and established the Mughal dynasty. It was Babur's grandson Akbar who finally brought a measure of political stability to the north.

The Mughal period is synonymous in the history of the subcontinent with some of the finest developments in art and architecture. Akbar's political policy of integrating disparate elements and forging alliances with Hindu Rajput kings, who had earlier been sworn enemies, was reflected in the aesthetic idiom that was created under the Mughals, with the fusion of Persian, Muslim and classical Hindu styles. The high point of Mughal architecture is, of course, the Taj Mahal, but each of the six great rulers of the dynasty can lay claim to memorable buildings and works of art.

The East India Company

At the turn of the 16th century, the entire subcontinent was divided into small warring fiefdoms, creating a certain amount of political instability. Vasco da Gama had already landed at Calicut in southern India in 1498, and tales of India's wealth had reached almost all parts of the world, including Europe. The Portuguese, the Dutch, the French and the British all wanted to establish colonies in India, although their motives ranged from the religious to the economic. The trade and other links between various European powers and Mughal India led to the British establishing the East India Company, which eventually extended its commercial interests to play a more political role in the subcontinent. By 1857, the last Mughal emperor had been deposed by the British, who had brought most of India under the dynasty's domination. Finally, India was declared to be a colony of Imperial Britain.

Two hundred years of colonial rule created a drastic schism in architectural developments. The Western rulers brought new concepts of building which they imposed on the traditional vocabulary. Broadly classified as the Colonial style, this became a hybrid manifestation of new and old structural forms and decorative elements. Public institutions such as railway stations, post offices and administrative centers entered the realm of building. Domestic architecture was typified by the bungalow. For nearly 5,000 years, the Indian subcontinent had lured outsiders who came to conquer but stayed and merged their identities and became a part of India. The British, however, remained outsiders, and their economic and political exploitation of the country finally ended in 1947 when India became independent. India's struggle for political freedom was largely peaceful even though independence was gained after the traumatic partition of India and the creation of Pakistan.

The modern phase in Indian architecture is still very young. Though Western masters of the 20th century such as Le Corbusier and Louis Kahn have left their imprint on the urban landscape, there is a growing debate among a new generation of Indian architects on tradition versus modernity and what is most relevant to India in the 21st century.

CALCUTTA MUSEUM

Residential Spaces

Traditional Indian households lived by the joint family system whereby the many occupants and complex interpersonal relationships necessitated clearly demarcated spaces. Public and private areas were separate, and women kept protected from the public gaze. The internal courtyard was the center, restricted to family members, with rooms opening out on either side, ensuring privacy to their inhabitants.

Above: The stone façades of *havelis* in Rajasthan. Ornate *jharokhas* (balconies) with wooden shuttered openings project out onto the street. They are shaded by arched *chhajjas* (eaves).

Below: Section of a typical *haveli* showing the hierarchy of private and public spaces and connecting passageways.

North India: The Haveli

The *haveli* or mansion was the house of the rich, owned by either the nobility or by rich traders who attempted to imitate the lifestyle of royalty. Often built on narrow streets, the outer walls of larger *havelis* rose 3–4 stories high, casting shadows on their neighbors. Interiors thus remained cool. The narrow streets also acted as wind funnels, further cooling the buildings.

The *haveli* was built on a high plinth, with steps leading up to the entrance. The first room, facing the street, was the *baithak* or public area. It signified the transition between the public space outside the house and the private or personal space within. This was a totally male

domain into which women rarely entered. The *baithak* opened out into another room, beyond which, completely shielded from the gaze of strangers, was the central courtyard.

A pillared and covered corridor called the *baramdah* or verandah ran around the courtyard on all levels, leading into various rooms that formed the living quarters. Rooms on the upper floors also had canopied balconies called *jharokhas* looking down into the street. Shielded by carved stone latticework screens (*jaalis*), they allowed the inhabitants to look out without being seen, and also served to break the force of hot winds, allowing the interiors to be airy. There was usually a *teh khana* or basement,

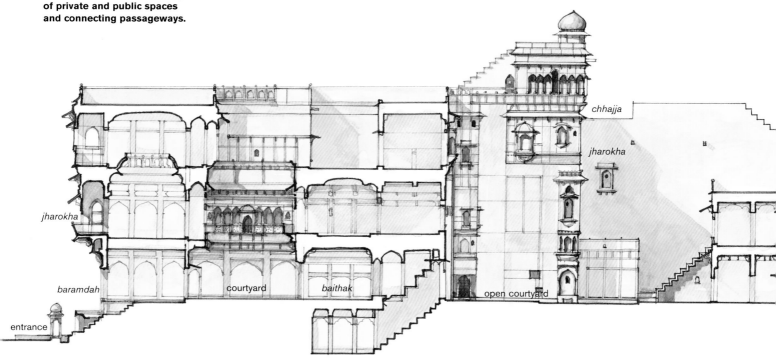

chhajja

jharokha

jharokha

baramdah   courtyard   baithak   open courtyard

entrance

which was the cool retreat of the house and also the place where valuables were stored. Security was, in fact, a major determinant in the plan. Doors had low lintels and high thresholds, probably to ensure that an unwelcome person could not enter easily. The staircases, too, were twisted and narrow, with uncomfortably high risers.

Ornamentation was a key feature of *havelis*. It also served as a major unifying element in the somewhat organic planning of the house. Owners of *havelis* vied with each other to create opulent mansions with painted interiors and ornate stone- and woodwork.

South India: The Kerala House

Homes in Kerala follow rigid systems of planning and orientation. The generic Kerala house is known as the *nalukettu*, *nalu* meaning "four" and *kettu* meaning "courtyard." The house thus comprises four blocks around a courtyard.

The courtyard, according to the *Vaastu Shastra* (see p. 30), is the point of equilibrium and harmony in the domestic building. It provides a focal point for the home. Based on this principle, the *nalukettu* is surrounded by a deep, covered verandah, whose inward-sloping roof rests on a pillar at each corner. Rooms are arranged around the verandah in a linear fashion. The roof is pitched and extends over the exterior walls to cover another verandah, usually in the front portion of the house.

Within this basic layout, the *tarawad* or house of the Hindu Nair community, follows rigid principles of orientation. A *tarawad* must face east, and the entrance is always flanked by the image of a demon to ward off evil spirits.

Within the *tarawad*, areas are designated according to direction. Thus, the cooking area, known as the *vadakkina*, must be in the north, while the southern end, known as the *tekkina*, is reserved for other domestic chores. The four blocks of the *tarawad* must be oriented in the cardinal directions around a central courtyard known as the *nadumuttam*.

The traditional Mappila or Muslim house of Kerala, has a central courtyard and is two-storied. The main entrance leads into a lobby or enclosed verandah, with a pair of windows opening through three arches giving onto the true verandah. The raised floor is paved with stone tile or colored lime plaster. Here stands a *kinathara*, a platform some 0.6 meters above floor level—a combined prayer area and sitting space. The rooms become plainer and more functional as one passes toward the women's quarter at the back, the most private part of the house. From one side of the semi-private lobby, stairs ascend to the finest room, the *mullapuram*.

The interior courtyard of a *nalukettu*. The courtyard is a transitional space between the public and private realms. Extended roofs provide much needed shade in the hot and rainy seasons.

Vernacular Architecture

India's rich diversity has given shape to an equally rich vocabulary of vernacular architecture. Just as political and historic events were major factors in shaping monumental buildings in India in the past, so geography, social customs, local materials and, above all, the climate have been important influences on the forms of personal living spaces.

Vernacular architecture evolved in an organic manner using local craft skills. It can broadly be divided into two distinct categories on the basis of the construction material used. The *kachcha* building is one that is made from short-lived natural materials such as mud, grass, bamboo, thatch and sticks and its form is dictated by the practical limitations of the material. Structures made with these materials have a short life and require constant upkeep and replenishment, not only in hostile weather conditions but throughout the year. They have the advantage, however, of being cheap. The *pukka* structure is one made from stone, burnt brick with plaster, seasoned timber, clay tiles or any other material that is resistant to wear and tear, and does not need constant repair and replenishment. Such structures, while being stronger, are much more

Interior of a village hut revealing clay relief work and pieces of mirror used for decoration. A further decorative element is often a quilted wall hanging.

expensive to build. As villagers' earnings increase, vernacular building, mainly confined to rural locations, combines these two types to create the semi-*pukka* structure. The dream of every villager is to finally own a *pukka* home although the *kachcha* structure has its own beauty, derived less from decoration (which is common due to religion or superstition) and more from its pure, practical shapes.

Diverse Materials

In the hills, the walls of houses are made of random rubble or ashlar, using bits of flint or stone, packed with mud mortar. A variation consists of a timber frame and bonding, with the space between columns filled with random rubble in mud mortar till the sill level and then with finer stonework. Wooden beams and rafters support roofs made of locally available slate tiles which are sloping, to drain off rain or snow.

In contrast, the roofs of houses in the plains are flat, allowing access to the terrace, used for sleeping in the hot summer. They are made of stone slabs supported on a metal framework. Walls are made of either mud or sun-baked brick, and plastered on the inside and outside with mud mixed with hay, chaff and cowdung, and sometimes whitewashed with lime (also considered a disinfectant).

Bamboo, flexible but extremely resilient, is used widely as material for walls, scaffolding,

platforms and floors in the northeastern region and in the eastern states of Bengal and Orissa. Thatch from various plants—coconut, paddy, elephant grass—is widely used all over the country as roofing material. In the south, clay tiles are the most common *pukka* roofing material. The structural material for construction in the south is usually casuarina or the coconut palm, good for roofing and roof beams. Floors can be either compacted earth, or laid with stone. Clay flooring with a traditional, painstakingly prepared red laterite polish is also commonly used in the south.

Variations in Form and Infrastructure
Homes in the hills are usually two-storied, with domestic animals occupying the ground floor and humans the first floor. This ensures safety for the livestock as well as warmth during the cold winter season. In many houses, a verandah runs along one side of the house, and on the upper floors this verandah projects out, resting on brackets or corbeled out. The attic is used to store grain, root vegetables, chillies and corn.

The roofs are always pitched, and in the northeast, with a very wet climate, have deep projecting eaves to prevent rainwater from damaging the walls. The plinths in this part are raised on bamboo poles, to counter floods.

In the high and dry plateau of Ladakh, the pitched roof gives way to a flat one with houses having more than one floor, built close to one another, with connecting passages.

In arid southern Rajasthan, mud is fashioned into dramatic shapes and the walls are rounded, allowing the desert winds to whistle past without damaging them. A cluster of structures faces a common courtyard. Rectangular forms are more common in the northern desert region.

On the west coast, fishing settlements have thatched roofs of coconut fronds or thick, dried paddy projecting over large verandahs, which can be used as a work space during the heavy monsoons.

Village homes have low lintels, made of either stone or wood, ensuring that whoever enters has to bow his head, which not only ensures safety from hostile strangers but is also a gesture of respect. Thick mud walls allow for windows and doors to be inset as well as for simple stone slab shelves to be fixed.

Left and opposite below: The villagers of Banni in the Kutch peninsula of Gujarat build circular houses of mud. A conical roof frame is filled in with thatch tightly tied around it. There are usually no windows. As families increase, new homes are built, eventually clustering around a common open space or internal courtyard. Decoration is an intrinsic part of the Banni house and includes mud relief, paint and embedded colored glass.

Above: Clay tiles are a popular roofing material for *pukka* roofs in South India.

Left: A typical hill house with a sloping tin roof.

Elements of Space and Decoration

Elaborate color-filled carvings constitute the façade elements in the *havelis* of Jaisalmer.

Modernity is but one of the many overlays that constitute the complex canvas of Indian lifestyles, and in every region the architectural features of buildings have deep cultural resonances of older ways of living. Traditional homes in India share certain spatial and ornamental elements which are common, regardless of where they are located The names of these elements may vary according to the region but their function and character are accepted as indispensable to domestic architecture, just as the *zenana* (women's quarters) was essential for reasons of *purdah* and distinct from the *mardana* (spaces restricted to men).

The Courtyard

The *Vaastu Shastra* defines the focal point of any building as the point of equilibrium. In the domestic dwelling, this is the courtyard, an enclosed private space, open to the sky. Present even in the earliest homes of the Indus valley civilisation, the courtyard is the major spatial element of homes in the plains. In Hindu households, there is a *tulsi* plant (holy basil) at its center, revered for its healing powers. It is usually contained within a plinth or ornate planter.

The Threshold

The threshold signifies the transition of space from the public to the private. In traditional buildings, the threshold is slightly elevated, both to prevent hostile intrusions as well as to keep out insects and reptiles. Footwear is removed at this point, and one enters the house barefoot.

The Hearth

The cooking hearth, known as the *chulha*, is the purest space in the traditional house. The area around the *chulha* is ritually washed before the preparation of the morning meal, and it is essential to bathe before entering it. The women of the house do all the cooking and serving. At all meals, the men are served first, sitting on low wooden stools called *chowkis*. Sometimes,

Not only within houses but between them courtyard-like spaces provide the public interactive area. In hot cities like Jaisalmer, narrow streets open up to provide areas for people to get together. Architectural features include *jharokhas* and decorated galleries.

a second *chulha* was constructed in the courtyard for boiling water and other purposes.

The *chulha* was designed to use firewood, and the smoke that rose from it was welcome as it killed vermin. Most houses did not have a chimney. In some tribal houses, the apex of the roof was open to the sky and covered by a clay pot that could be lifted when required.

Decorative Elements

The Indian love for color and design is evident in even the humblest of homes. Floors, especially in the areas around the threshold and the family

shrine, are decorated with patterns drawn with rice flour, powdered chalk, flower petals or turmeric powder. This ritual decoration, called *kolam*, *rangoli* or *alpana*, whether done daily or for special occasions, is evident throughout the country, although the patterns executed differ from place to place. Walls are also painted or molded in relief with both geometric and iconographic motifs.

Most homes had small niches built into the wall, like the *mihrab* in mosques, used to keep candles or lamps, to house a shrine, or simply for storage. Kutch homes are covered with such ornate niches. The ornamentation in larger Hindu homes depicted entire scenes, involving figures and deities from mythology, the epics and stories from the *Puranas*. Usually the location and the subject of the paintings followed a set order. Entrances had auspicious symbols painted on them. The colors used were earth colors. Communities of fresco painters traditionally trained in the art were employed to execute elaborate designs by wealthy patrons.

Structural elements were also exploited for decoration, such as the carved or latticed *jharokhas* of Rajasthan, brackets and pillars.

Top left: The interior of a hut in Kutch shows the women's decorative handiwork with mirrors and relief abstract.

Top right: Frescoes of religious or mythological scenes adorn the walls of *havelis* of the rich merchant class in Mandawa, Rajasthan.

Above: An example of Ladakhi wooden pillar capitals painted with bright Tibetan and Chinese motifs which support the ceiling of a traditional house.

Below left: Unlike the permanent decorations painted on the façade and on spatially important parts of the house, paintings with washable materials at the entry point celebrate important rituals or festive events, either within the house or outside in the overall context of the community.

Architecture and Science

Indian literary sources provide evidence of the deep and close relationship ancient India had with numerals and other branches of science. Astronomy and astrology were important preoccupations and the building treatise, *Vaastu Shastra*, relies on calculations based on cosmogony and religious abstract theory. Later examples manifest more overtly the relationship between architecture and the sciences.

Sawai Jai Singh II, the 18th-century ruler of Jaipur, was a keen scholar, statesman and astronomer, who was inspired by the works of Mirza Ulugh Beg, the astronomer-king of Samarkand. He built five observatories, called the Jantar Mantar, in the northern cities of Delhi, Ujjain, Varanasi, Mathura and Jaipur.

A perfect blend of function and aesthetics makes these buildings unique creations. A collector of Western scientific instruments, Jai Singh was convinced that the available instruments were not adequate to achieve the degree of accuracy he sought in building observatories.

Instead of placing instruments within them, he therefore designed the structures themselves as instruments. Elegant futuristic forms were created by combining various geometrical shapes—hemispheres, arcs, cylinders, cubes and triangles. Until as recently as the advent of the satellite, these structures were used to predict certain meteorological phenomena.

Jantar Mantar, Jaipur

The Jantar Mantar in Jaipur is the largest and best preserved of Jai Singh's five observatories. Built between 1728 and 1734 in red sandstone,

South of the City Palace in Jaipur, the Jantar Mantar (literally "instrument to make calculations") was the most ambitious of Jai Singh II's observatories. It looks like a futuristic playground.

it is set in a large garden and consists of sixteen different large-scale instruments or *yantras*. Of these instruments, the Laghu Samrat Yantra can calculate Jaipur's local time up to an accuracy of 20 seconds. The Chakra Yantra is used to determine the angle of stars and planets from the equator. The Ram Yantra observes the celestial arc between the horizon and the zenith, and also measures the sun's altitude. The Jai Prakash Yantra, believed to be Jai Singh's own invention, verifies the accuracy of the other instruments. The Rashivalaya Yantra is composed of twelve pieces, each representative of a zodiac sign. It is used to cast horoscopes. The 23-meter-high Samrat Yantra is used to forecast the year's rainfall.

Jantar Mantar, Delhi

The Jantar Mantar complex in New Delhi, now obsolete, is located in the heart of the city, in a pleasant park surrounded by high-rise buildings. Built in 1724 and made of red brick and plaster, on a smaller scale than the Jaipur observatory, the structure is popular with tourists.

Above left: The Jantar Mantar in the heart of Delhi is a popular tourist attraction.

Above right: The Rashivalaya Yantra, made up of twelve pieces, each facing a different constellation, was used by astrologers to make horoscopes.

Left: The Ram Yantra was one of two identical structures used to calculate the celestial arc from horizon to zenith, as well as the altitude of the sun.

Also in the Jaipur observatory, the Unnatansha Yantra was used to determine the position of the celestial bodies at any time of the day or night.

Architecture and Water

Indian cosmology perceives water as a purifying and regenerative element, and it is an essential part of prayer and consecration. Water is also held in reverence because of its scarcity in many parts of the country. India depends on the monsoon rains to replenish its water sources and for irrigation. Failure of the monsoon means death and famine to many, while its timely arrival is an occasion for rejoicing.

Adalaj Vav, built in 1499 by Rudabai, the wife of a local chieftain, is covered with sculptures of dancing maidens, erotica and images of Shiva. It comprises a series of platforms and galleries raised on pillars on the sides of the stepwell.

Rani-ki-vav at Patan, Gujarat's largest stepwell, was built in 1050 in the Solanki period and extensively restored in the 1980s.

The sacredness of water finds acknowledgment throughout the subcontinent through extraordinary and monumental architecture that displays the acme of engineering achievement.

Stepwells or Vav

The concept of the *vav*, or stepwell, was a response to the harsh climate of Gujarat and Rajasthan in the west of India and the acute shortage of water. Since wells access groundwater, they are the most reliable source of a continuous water supply. The best examples of the *vav* in Gujarat are those created by the Solanki kings in the 12th and 13th centuries. Later, the Muslim rulers of the state carried on this architectural tradition.

The *vav* came to be associated with more than just a water source. The architecture around the original well was designed in such a way that the *vav* came to be a subterranean retreat. The *vav* consists of two elements. The well itself is a vertical shaft with a thick surrounding wall to maximize water retention. A series of imposing flights of steps, built over an inclined passage, broken at various regular levels by landings, leads from the ground level to the water level deep below.

The flights of steps, built between two massive retaining walls, are covered at various levels, as are the series of pillared galleries and chambers that open out from each landing. The Rani-ki-Vav at Patan, which descends to seven stories beneath the ground level and measures 36 meters by 4 meters, gives an idea of the scale. Pillars, capitals, railings and walls, all made of local stone, are sumptuously carved, with a mixture of decorative motifs and iconography, creating a unique architecture.

Reservoirs and Tanks (Kunds)

A combination of practical water storage with pleasure and palaces on the one hand, and with temples and rituals on the other, is common in Indian water architecture. The balance of sacred and royal aspects is different at every site. In Rajasthan, the temple tank or *kund* takes the form of a deep storage basin with long and narrow flights of stairs leading down to deep reservoirs. The design of these tanks combines the cooling features of wells with those of a water basin conducive to purification rituals.

Ghats

The *ghat*, meaning "riverbank" or "steps leading to water," is a common feature of many temples situated on the banks of rivers. In Hinduism, every river is representative of the Ganges, believed to flow out of the hair of the god Shiva, and whose waters are therefore considered to be most sacred.

Hindus believe that death in this life is but a stage in the journey of the soul. Hence the

ashes of those who are cremated are immersed in the waters of sacred rivers, to mark the beginning of this onward journey. The *ghat* provides the physical place to commemorate this, and some of India's most colorful architecture has developed along the banks of sacred rivers, in joyous but respectful celebration of the journey of the soul.

The *ghats* at Varanasi (Benares) are the most sacred. The city derives its name from the two *ghats* that mark its extremes. The Varana Ghat is located at one end of the nearly 4-kilometer stretch that ends at the Asi Ghat. The riverfront is bordered by steps that lead down to the river, interspersed with temples, *chhattris* and shrines, palaces, *dharamshalas* or pilgrim shelters, and other buildings. These *ghats* were built over many hundreds of years by royal and noble patrons. Amongst the nearly 80 *ghats* that constitute the architecture of the Varanasi riverfront, the Manikarnika Ghat is specially devoted to cremation rites.

Water Palaces and Pavilions

The bathing pool at the northern end of the Jahaz Mahal at Mandu.

The Deeg Water Palace, once a romantic summer retreat for the Jat kings of Bharatpur. It is a fine example of the skill with which an elaborate cooling system was devised, drawing water from a huge reservoir.

In the hot, arid climate of the northern plains, the onset of the monsoon is associated with intense pleasure and is a time of celebration. This joy and exuberance has found expression in music, art, literature and, of course, architecture. In many palaces and forts, specially designed pavilions and terraces were created with the express purpose of enjoying the rain and cool moisture-laden breeze.

The Water Palace, Deeg

Perhaps the most extravagant tribute to the magic of the monsoon is the Water Palace built by Raja Suraj Mal of Bharatpur in the late 18th century. The palace is located at Deeg, where the Bharatpur kings had their summer capital, and is an elaborate complex of marble and sandstone pavilions, a large tank, pools, fountains, waterways and gardens.

The complex is built within a *charbagh* (paradise garden) comprising a central octagonal pool with fountains, from which four paved pathways lead to the various pavilions and palaces. Two tanks flank the complex. A huge reservoir, that originally took two days to fill, feeds the elaborate network of water channels that form part of the cooling system of the palace complex. The various palaces and

pavilions contain many ingenious ways to experience the rain and to simulate the monsoon.

The months of Sawan (July) and Bhadon (August), when the monsoon is at its strongest, lend their names to two pavilions that project out over the Gopal Sagar tank. They are roofed over with a sandstone replica of the *bangla* roof (see p. 87), which contains a clever water system creating a semicircular arc of falling water. The pavilions flank the Gopal Bhawan, the main palace situated by the tank, making it look as if it is rising out of the water.

An elegant pavilion, the Keshav Bhawan, overlooks the Roop Sagar tank on the other side of the complex. It is a flat-roofed building with deep projecting eaves or *chhajjas* resting on symmetrically placed pillars with arched openings. The pillars are hollow and within them run pipes which continue within the structure over the arches. Heavy stone balls used to be placed on the roof so that when water gushed up through the pipes, these stone balls rolled to produce the sound of thunder.

The Nand Bhawan, another palace, uses a traditional, indigenous method to keep its interiors cool. Between its double roof are sandwiched upturned earthen water pitchers that serve the function of insulation. Fountains sprayed jets of colored water that created rainbows. Immense marble urns filled with water and a number of small pools further enhanced the enjoyment of water.

The Jahaz Mahal, Mandu

The Jahaz Mahal, or Ship Palace (see p. 98), was built in the 15th century by Ghiyas-ud-Din Khalji, much of whose 30-year reign was spent in amusement and pleasure. Standing on a narrow strip of land between two lakes, it is 122 meters long and a little over 15 meters wide. The façade is about 10 meters in height.

The lower part of the building has a series of continuous arcades, over which rests a wide *chhajja* on stone corbels. The upper part is articulated by a series of built-in arches over which runs a wide parapet decorated with glazed tile, in the typical provincial style of the region. The ground floor consists of three huge halls separated by corridors, with small

enclosures at the extremities. At the rear of each hall, a small pavilion projects out into the lake.

The central pavilion is the largest and has a domed ceiling decorated with blue and yellow tiles. The other smaller pavilions were meant for the harem, and one can still see the stone frameworks that were used to hang curtains to ensure privacy. The room at one of the extremities has a channel from which the cistern was filled. The cistern was used also as a swimming pool. It has an elegant shape, and is one of the special features of the palace. On the upper floor is another cistern, fed with water through elegant spiral-shaped channels.

The island palace of Jag Nivas, Udaipur, now converted into the Lake Palace Hotel, was built between 1743 and 1746.

In a pavilion at Mandu, spring water from the rockface crosses the marble floor in an inlaid channel and cascades down before it reaches a square pool, then exits through a delicate spiral.

Water within Architecture

Even though the presence of water in the form of temple tanks had been a part of sacred architecture in India for many centuries, it was really the Mughals who perfected extraordinary ways of integrating it within the building. The concept of the *charbagh* had originated with Babur and found its most perfect expression in both Humayun's Tomb and the Taj Mahal, and in the pleasure gardens of Kashmir. Evolving from the fountains and channels of the *charbagh*, Mughal architects designed a system of water courses that ran under the building, creating an elaborate network of waterways that kept the floor cool during summer. In the Rang Mahal of Delhi's Red Fort, built by Shah Jahan, the main water channel that brought the water from the River Yamuna, along whose banks it was built, wove its way through the complex. Known as the Nahar-i-Bahisht or Stream of Paradise, the channel fed a warren of smaller channels that ran underground. Within the *zenana* of the Rang Mahal, this channel cascaded over a sloped and carved marble ramp to end in a shallow marble pool sculpted in the shape of a flattened, fully blooming lotus (see p. 114). From each petal of the flower spurted a jet of water, so that the petals and inlaid leaves seemed to move gently with the ripples.

Early Architecture

The beginnings of Indian architecture can be traced back to as early as the 3rd millennium BC, to the architecture of the civilisation that flourished in the valley of the Indus River. Archaeological excavations undertaken in the Indus valley have revealed the existence of well-planned cities, broad roads, excellent sanitation systems and the use of bricks in construction.

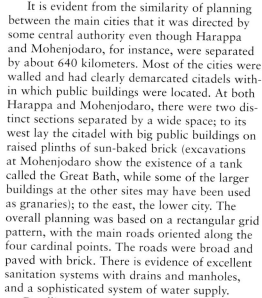

The 10-centimeter-tall "dancing girl" figure excavated at Mohenjodaro, now in the National Museum in Delhi.

Lothal, a flourishing seaport around 2440 BC on the Gulf of Cambay, was excavated in 1954. A mud-brick wall surrounds the rectangular site. Wide streets intersect and divide the town into smaller blocks, typical of cities and towns of the Indus valley.

The Indus valley civilisation (also referred to as the Harappa civilisation) extended west to east from northern Afghanistan to the Gangetic plain, and north to south from the Himalayan foothills to the Gulf of Cambay.

Indus Valley Excavations

Excavations carried out in the Indus valley sites of the two great cities, Mohenjodaro and Harappa, now in Pakistan, and at Dholavira and Lothal in Gujarat, India, show the existence of well laid out cities and towns, designed according to a predetermined common code of planning principles which formed the basis of urban design. These cities and townships were originally designed specifically as urban centers, and did not evolve from small hamlets or groups of dwellings.

It is evident from the similarity of planning between the main cities that it was directed by some central authority even though Harappa and Mohenjodaro, for instance, were separated by about 640 kilometers. Most of the cities were walled and had clearly demarcated citadels within which public buildings were located. At both Harappa and Mohenjodaro, there were two distinct sections separated by a wide space; to its west lay the citadel with big public buildings on raised plinths of sun-baked brick (excavations at Mohenjodaro show the existence of a tank called the Great Bath, while some of the larger buildings at the other sites may have been used as granaries); to the east, the lower city. The overall planning was based on a rectangular grid pattern, with the main roads oriented along the four cardinal points. The roads were broad and paved with brick. There is evidence of excellent sanitation systems with drains and manholes, and a sophisticated system of water supply.

Dwelling units, both big, almost resembling palaces, as well as small, were rectangular and planned around a square courtyard. The entrances of houses opened out onto small side streets rather than the main thoroughfares.

Most of the buildings were made of standardised kiln-baked brick, with sun-baked bricks used to construct plinths and flooring. Archaeological evidence also reveals that the size of the brick was standard across all the sites, which also indicates that there must have been close and sustained contact between the various cities of the civilisation. Mud mortar was used in the construction of walls, and mud plaster for inner walls and surfaces. Staircases and the thickness of the walls indicate that many of the buildings were two-storied structures, with the upper floor probably made of wood.

Excavations have also unearthed a number of objects, from seals, urns and pots to jewelry, statuettes, toys and agricultural implements. The

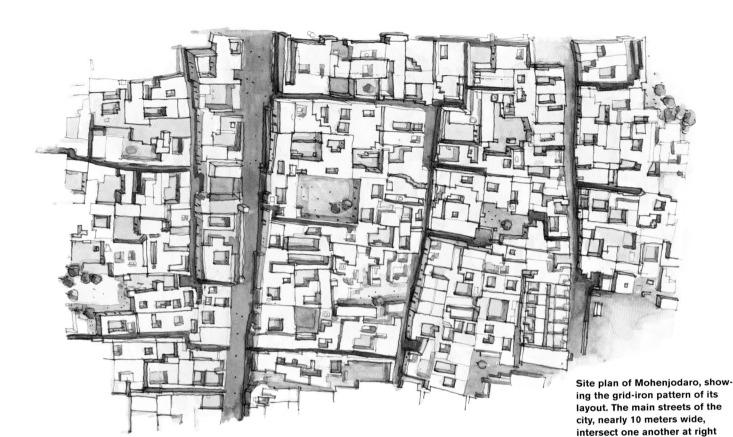

Site plan of Mohenjodaro, showing the grid-iron pattern of its layout. The main streets of the city, nearly 10 meters wide, intersect one another at right angles, dividing the city into rectangular blocks.

seals carry inscriptions in a script yet to be deciphered, as well as elaborate intaglio designs depicting animals, plants, human figures and geometric motifs. Some statuettes depict the mother goddess, embodying fertility. Among the stone sculptures, those of the "priest-king" and the "dancing girl" are well known. The "priest-king" is a steatite bust of a bearded male with half-closed eyes that were once inlaid with shell. The slender "dancing girl" adopts a bold posture, one hand on hip and head tilted back.

All the architectural evidence points to the Indus valley civilisation having been a conservative but sophisticated and homogeneous society with a centralised system of governance. It had a thriving economy based on agriculture and internal as well as external trade.

Decline of the Indus Valley Civilisation

The civilisation went into sudden decline in the 2nd millennium BC. The causes for the decline remain a mystery, although various hypotheses have been forwarded by historians and archaeologists alike. Flooding of the Indus valley and climatic changes drastically affecting agricultural output are among the many reasons given. A more widely accepted one is that diverse tribes originating from Central Asia began to enter India around this time, through mountain passes in the northwestern Himalayas via Persia (Iran). These tribes, called the Indo-Aryans, had origins in common with other fair-skinned tribes inhabiting Europe. They were a nomadic people dependent on cattle, and they worshipped a wide range of natural phenomena, including the sun, the wind and fire. The Indo-Aryans subjugated the native inhabitants and gradually settled into agrarian communities, accepting and assimilating some of the practices of the natives, especially those of worship.

A toy cart made of terracotta, excavated from Harappa. Objects such as this have been used by archaeologists as evidence to prove that the streets were wide enough for vehicular traffic.

The Vaastu Shastra

By about 1100 BC, the Indo-Aryans had settled in India. The Aryan traditions were enshrined in a series of compositions called the *Vedas*, which were transmitted orally for over a millennium. Nothing survives of the architecture of the Vedic age before the 3rd century BC. However, evidence of architectural activity is available from literary sources of the period.

A representation of the *Vaastu Purusha Mandala* showing the seated form of Brahma or the Creator within a square. The concept of the *mandala* (cosmic diagram) is universal and can be applied equally to a temple, house, city, or indeed the entire universe. The center of the *mandala* is the point of convergence of all energies. In temples, this corresponds to the position of the *sanctum sanctorum*, while in a residence, it is the central open courtyard.

The Aryan Tradition of Worship

The *Rig Veda*, the earliest of the Aryan *Vedas*, is a collection of hymns glorifying the power of the sacrificial ritual. The Hindu pantheon of gods was first written about here. Mount Meru, later called Mount Kailasha, was the abode in the mountains where the gods dwelt, ruled over by Varuna, guardian of the cosmic order. Surya was the sun god, Agni the god of fire, Indra the god of war, Yama the god of death and Soma the god of vitality. The original religion as expressed in the *Vedas* was Brahmanism, but it evolved to what we know as Hinduism today, which has been practiced, in more or less same form, for over 3,000 years.

Each god was associated with a symbol, and these symbols form an important part of Hinduism's religious and architectural iconography. The process of worship was expressed architecturally by the *chaitya*, or the sacred place or object of worship, and the sacrificial altar or *veyaddi*, where ritualistic offerings of flowers and food were made.

From the literary sources of the period, ranging from the *Vedas* and the *Upanishads* to the two great epic poems of the age, the *Mahabharata* and the *Ramayana*, we know that the Aryans cremated the dead, and that all buildings were built according to certain basic principles of Brahmanism, governed by the *Vaastu Shastra* and, most importantly, of perishable materials, which is why no evidence remains of these buildings. The literature speaks of the use of materials like timber, bamboo and thatch. Brick and mud were also used, but the thatch hut seems to have been the predominant architectural typology of the Vedic age.

The early Vedic temple is likely to have been a thatched or wooden structure in which the altar was placed. The concept of sacrifice and worship of fire defined the altar, which was considered to be the microcosm of the sacred space.

The Vaastu Shastra

The power of sacrifice, its architectural expression and design of the sacred space, were strictly codified in the *Vaastu Shastra*, or the treatise on the science of building and orientation. It is based on the fundamental premise that on earth or soil is a living organism out of which other living creatures and organic forms emerge.

Vaastu means "dwelling place," or indeed any planned building, and *shastra* means "science" or "knowledge." The *Vaastu Shastra* is a highly complex set of rules and regulations that formulate a system of orientation, site planning, plans and proportions of buildings, the iconography to be used and the links between these physical elements and metaphysical rhythms, establishing the harmony between natural and supernatural forces. The actual plan of the building was based on the *Vaastu Purusha Mandala*. *Purusha* means "man," personified as the Creator, later known as Brahma, and *mandala* means "cosmic diagram."

The Vaastu Purusha Mandala

The *Vaastu Purusha Mandala* shows the position of Brahma or the Creator within a square. According to Vedic cosmology, the circle represents the

earth, chaos and irrational nature, while the square represents the heavens, order and rational thought. Each side of the square can be further divided into as many as 32 units. The subdivisions indicate the four cardinal directions, the position of the eight planets, the seasons of the year and the direction of the sun.

The diagonals of the square divide the *mandala* into triangles, and within the basic square more circles can be inscribed. The center of the *mandala*, which represents harmony and equilibrium, is indicated by the Purusha's navel, and each part of his body within the *mandala* represents a part of the building to be designed. Elaborate mathematical formulae govern the square, circle and triangle and their subdivisions, as well as their correlation and symbolism in depicting the universe.

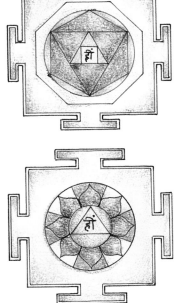

Above left: Early rock-cut shrine at Gwalior Fort.

Above: The *paramasayika mandala* (above), with 9 x 9 units of squares, and (below) the *manduka mandala*, with 8 x 8 units of squares.

Left: Sculpture of the snake spirit (*naga*) often worshipped under the *peepal* (*Ficus religiosa*) tree.

Sacred Buddhist Spaces

The philosophical questions posed in the *Upanishads* on the relationship between the individual and the Universe, made them the basis for several heterodox religions which deviated from the Vedic roots of Hinduism. These included Buddhism, founded by Siddhartha Gautama, prince of Magadha, in the 6th century BC. By the 3rd century AD, Buddhism had become a major religion of India.

Stone cutting was brought to India in the 3rd century BC, and Buddhist architecture was the first to use stone as a building material.

Buddhist religious architecture, which flourished under the patronage of Emperor Ashoka, reflects the concept of meditation and worship, integral to the religion's rituals of prayer. It can be classified into three main types, based on the three cornerstones of Buddhism: first, the Buddha, an object of veneration, architecturally expressed in the *stupa*; second, the Dharma or religion, based on worship, which found expression in *chaitya* halls or sanctuaries; and third, the Sangha or community of monks, whose monasteries were called *vihara*.

The Stupa

The word *stupa* derives from the Sanskrit *stup* meaning "to heap." The earliest surviving form of religious architecture in India, the *stupa* was a funerary mound of earth and rubble, first erected to enshrine the cremated remains of the Buddha himself. Later, any holy relic associated with the religion, as well as the remains of some of the Buddha's disciples, came to be buried under similar structures, which were finished with brick and acquired a more ornamental form with the addition of *chhattris* (umbrellas surmounting the top) and railings (*vedika*). In the course of time, innumerable *stupas* were built, some merely votive in character and small

Detail from a gateway, now in the Mathura Museum.

The *Mahastupa* or Great Stupa, built in the 1st century BC at Sanchi in central India, is the largest among several *stupas* and temples of varying sizes. A century later, it was enlarged to nearly twice its size. It now stands 36 meters in diameter and 16.5 meters in height. Its four *toranas*, each 8.5 meters high, were originally made of wood. The stone replicas were added later. The *pradak-shina patha* is divided into two, with an outer *patha* at ground level, defined by a massive unadorned stone *vedika*, and a staircase or *so-pana*. This leads directly to the inner *patha*, raised on a drum, which encircles the *anda* (dome) of the *stupa*.

enough to be carried by Buddhist pilgrims. Emperor Ashoka himself is said to have built 84,000 *stupas*, of which the one at Sanchi (3rd century BC) is the best known. In its original form it gradually fell into disrepair and was only discovered in the early 19th century when major restoration work by the British resulted in its present condition. Other well-known *stupas* in India include those at Bharhut, Sarnath and Nagarjunakonda, culminating in the Great Stupa at Amravati, where only the base remains.

Thus, the *stupa* itself gradually became an object of veneration and worship. A solid structure, with no means to enter it, unlike other funerary monuments such as the pyramids of Egypt, the *stupa* has its own intricate and complex iconography and philosophy of form.

Elements of the Stupa

The hemispherical dome of the *stupa*, known as the *anda*, stands for the dome of heaven. The circular plan is symbolic of the wheel, as a regulator of cosmic time, as also a representation of the lotus. The central cosmic axis is emphasised by a finial, usually in the shape of a flat disk called a *chhattri* or umbrella. The *chhattri* is also an expression of honor to the Buddha, signifying protection and representing the Bodhi Tree. It is supported on a mast known as the *yasti*. Sometimes a series of *chhattris*, the whole known as the *chattravali*, defines the apex of the *stupa*. A square railing near the summit, called the *harmika*, defines the space taken up, according to the plan, by the holy relic buried within the *stupa*.

An integral part of the Buddhist ritual of worship is to walk clockwise around the *stupa* with the right shoulder turned toward it as a mark of reverence. This circumambulation is meant to be a re-enactment of the rotational movement of celestial bodies, and also indicative of time in its cosmic sense. The paved path around the base of the *stupa* where this takes place is called the *pradakshina patha*, and this is enclosed by a fence or balustrade called the *vedika*. Sometimes the *stupa* has more than one *pradakshina patha*. The upper *pradakshina patha* is reached by a stone staircase called the *sopana*. Elaborate gateways called *torana* mark the four cardinal points at the corners of the *vedika*. The *stupa* is built of earth with an outer covering made of non-perishable material such as brick or brick-like stone. The *vedika*, *harmika* and *chhattri* are made of stone. The earliest *stupas* relied on austere simplicity and massive size to inspire awe, while later examples are intricately carved.

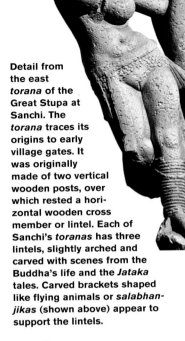

Detail from the east *torana* of the Great Stupa at Sanchi. The *torana* traces its origins to early village gates. It was originally made of two vertical wooden posts, over which rested a horizontal wooden cross member or lintel. Each of Sanchi's *toranas* has three lintels, slightly arched and carved with scenes from the Buddha's life and the *Jataka* tales. Carved brackets shaped like flying animals or *salabhanjikas* (shown above) appear to support the lintels.

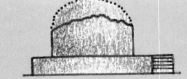
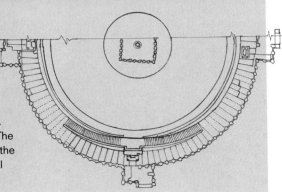

Evolution of the Stupa

The early form of the *stupa* (left), made of mud and brick, was austere and simple, relying on size and purity of form to aspire to the monumental. It was an architectural representation of the Buddha and therefore an object of veneration in itself. Gradually, the *stupa* evolved from its simple hemispherical shape into a more complex form (middle). The cylindrical base or drum on which the *stupa* was erected was heightened and niches with votive figures were incorporated. The pure hemispherical *anda* also became more bulbous. Smaller votive *stupas* were added clustering around the main *stupa*. The *harmika* and the *chhattri* began to merge, to create a ringed, spire-like ornate form. The *vedika* and the *torana* also became more ornate (right, including plan). In the Himalayas, the *stupa* was represented by the form called a *chorten* (see p. 41) to create an architectural language more specific to the locale.

The interior of a *chaitya* hall at Ajanta, early 8th century AD, with its carved stone imitation of a wooden barrel vault.

Entrance (below) and vertical section (below right) of the *chaitya* hall at Karli.

The Chaitya

The original *chaitya* hall of worship (from the Vedic *chaiti*, meaning "sacred place") or sanctuary for worship, was probably just a wooden shed with a thatched roof and a small *stupa* at one end. However, during the monsoon this proved to be inadequate shelter, and the monastic congregation found it necessary to move to places that offered better protection. This they sought in natural caves, used by ascetics (*sadhu*) for centuries. These caves, known as *varshavatika* or rain shelters, were the first examples of the permanent *chaitya*. The logical development from these to rock-cut architecture marks one of the most characteristic architectural traditions of India.

The earliest examples of rock-cut *chaitya* halls date back to about the 3rd century BC. Clues to the process of rock cutting are available at the unfinished caves. The process started at ceiling level and moved down, thus eliminating the need for scaffolding in the early stages. Many categories of workers and types of skill were employed in the process: rock cutters who did the initial removal of the rock, masons who executed the more precise cutting, and sculptors and polishers who performed the final finishing.

The basic plan consisted of a hall deep into the cave ending in an apse containing a *stupa*, with space around it for circumambulation. The roof was barrel-vaulted with the ribs of the wooden prototype clearly replicated in stone. The pillars used to support the beams of the original prototype were also replicated faithfully, though they were of no structural value in these essentially sculpted stone buildings. These stone replicas are evidence that ancient India had a well-developed tradition of wooden architecture.

The openings of the *chaitya* or entrance portals had sculpted façades, and were defined by a horseshoe arch reminiscent of the leaf of the Bodhi Tree (locally known as the *peepul*) under which the Buddha is believed to have gained Enlightenment. This motif of the Bodhi Tree was appropriated and later used in Hindu architecture as well.

Later examples of rock-cut *chaityas* show the development of the basic and rudimentary plan into an elaborate and complex arrangement of interlocking chambers, but with the basic elements of space and form still intact. The main hall evolved into a wide central bay flanked by rows of pillars demarcating side aisles. The single central chamber often had a number of smaller chambers opening off it, carved deep into the rock. The pillars, initially with plain bases and capitals, came to be profusely decorated with elaborate figures in bas as well as high relief, the iconography a mixture of Buddhist and pre-Vedic lore.

The Vihara

The *vihara* or monastery, an expression of the Sangha or community, was essentially residential in function. It comprised a series of cells where monks could live and meditate. Whether rock-cut or freestanding, the *vihara* consisted of a central courtyard surrounded by pillared halls and individual cells. Within the *vihara* was the *stupa* as well as the *chaitya*. There were separate

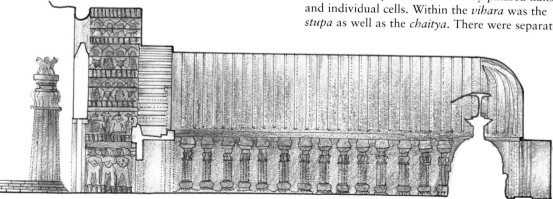

monasteries for monks and nuns. The free-standing *vihara* was built of stone or brick, and often over a long period of time. A cluster of several monasteries was called a *mahavihara*. By the 6th century, the *mahavihara* were famous as centers of great learning and liberal thought, attracting scholars and travelers from distant lands to participate in studies and discourses held at the monasteries.

Bihar state in the northeast is most closely associated with Buddhist architecture (the word Bihar itself derives from *vihara*). Here are located Bodh Gaya, where the Buddha achieved Enlightenment, marked by the Mahabodhi Temple sited over an original *vihara*; Rajgir, where Prince Siddhartha spent time after he renounced his royal state and which is on the way to Nalanda; and Vaishali, where the remains of a monastery, a *stupa* and a *chaitya* hall can still be found.

Left and below: Nalanda, in Bihar, is the finest and best known example of a *mahavihara* or monastic university. Spread over an area of 14 hectares, the ruins of Nalanda include eleven monasteries, five temples and three intricately carved stone pillars, an example of the artistic achievements of the Gupta age. The foundations of Nalanda were laid in the 5th century, when the first monastery was built. Over the next century, five more were built, and Nalanda continued to enjoy the patronage of successive Gupta kings (4th–6th centuries AD). Made of brick and stone, Nalanda today is a series of ruins; nevertheless, all the salient features of a *vihara* can still be seen. Individual cells are grouped together around a series of courtyards. In the center of each courtyard are the remains of a votive *stupa*. The dominant feature of Nalanda is the main *stupa* or temple No. 3, made of brick and stucco, at the southern end of the complex. The product of several phases of construction, it rises to a height of about 40 meters, and is decorated with stucco architectural moldings and niches containing stone figures of the Buddha and Bodhisattvas.

The Rock-cut Architecture of Ajanta

Above and below: Detail from a wall mural depicting a scene from the *Vishvantara Jataka*, that tells the story of a prince who gave away all his belongings in alms. The scene provides interesting information about contemporary wooden architecture, dress habits, and insights into courtly life.

Located in the Western Ghats (mountain ranges) of the Deccan, the horseshoe-shaped site of Ajanta was built under the patronage of the Vakataka king Harisena, who reigned from AD 460 to 478. Discovered in 1819 by a party of British army officers on a tiger hunt, the site consists of a series of 30 carved caves, some unfinished, which were excavated during a brief but intense period of activity. Cut into the sheer vertical mountainside above the Waghora River, many of the Ajanta caves are examples of major achievements of architecture, sculpture and painting. They contain several *chaitya* halls, shrines and *vihara* of the Mahayana Buddhist monks who lived there. Formerly accessed from the riverfront by individual staircases, the caves, numbered in terms of access from the entrance, are now connected by a terraced pathway.

Compared to earlier rock-cut architecture, the Ajanta caves are profusely decorated with sculptures and relief work, intricately carved

pilasters and cornices. Essentially still replicating wooden architecture, they show the evolution and development of the technique of integrating architecture with painting and sculpture, an integral feature of Indian architecture.

Some of the caves also contain exquisite murals on the dressed stone interiors, on walls and ceilings. Murals and sculptures depict the Buddha and Bodhisattvas, and scenes from his life, as illustrated in the *Jataka* tales.

Mural Techniques

The unpolished stone surfaces of the caves were first covered with mud plaster, and then with a lime wash which was allowed to dry before outlined sketches were drawn in red paint. The colors used for painting the murals on walls and ceilings were made of local minerals. A clay and iron oxide mixture was the source for red and yellow. Lapis lazuli, imported from Afghanistan, was used for blue. Kaolin, lamp-black and white lime were also used.

Often it was modulation of color rather than a hard outline that was used to create a form, which was then emphasised by techniques of shading and highlighting. Representation of the foreground as the lower part of the painting and the background as the higher part (a technique employed in earlier forms of sculptural relief),

Hinayana and Mahayana Buddhism

Hinayana (or the Lesser Vehicle), the earlier form of Buddhism, believes that Buddha-hood or Enlightenment can be achieved by only a few beings. Mahayana (or the Greater Vehicle) Buddhism accepts that the seed of Buddhahood is within each human being, and that it can be achieved by prayer, meditation and by following the Eightfold Path. The Buddha was not represented in human form in Hinayana Buddhism but through symbols such as the *stupa*, the Bodhi Tree or the lotus. Mahayana Buddhism gave the Buddha a human form, and created a rich vocabulary of representation of not only the Buddha but also the Bodhisattvas.

The crescent-shaped gorge of the Waghora River provided an ideal setting for Buddhist monks seeking a retreat. A series of caves, monastic dormitories and prayer halls were carved into the hillside. The caves seem to have been abandoned for almost a millennium before they were accidently discovered in 1819 by a group of British officers.

was continued in the Ajanta murals. An increasing use of perspective, too, is evident in the manner in which buildings are depicted.

There are significant differences in the formats of the ceiling and wall murals. The paintings on the ceilings generally have a grid pattern with floral and abstract patterns, while the wall murals are narrative. The ceilings are brightly colored with an abundant use of white, probably so that light could be reflected better (only diffused rays of sun penetrate the caves). The wall murals have predominantly earth tones; white is used sparingly. A number of styles and techniques may be discerned in the Ajanta murals, sometimes within the same composition, suggesting that large murals were a collaborative effort.

Site plan of the Ajanta Caves, most of which were *viharas* with cells placed around a central courtyard.

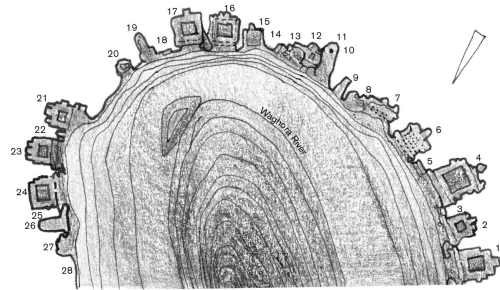

The sculptures in the Ajanta caves depict tales from the life of the Buddha, as well as the lives of the Buddha in his previous births, often sourced from the *Jatakas*. The sculpture here, from Cave 26, shows a 9-meter figure of the Parinirvana Buddha reclining on his right side between two *saal* trees. Above are the celestial beings and below are figures of the Buddha's followers mourning his death.

Building in the Himalayas

The Tawang Monastery in Sikkim is the second oldest Buddhist monastery in the world. Among the numerous murals at Tawang is this wall painting which depicts the Wheel of Life.

Ground floor plan of the Hemis Monastery. Public spaces were always located on the ground level of monasteries while residential areas were above.

The Gompa (Monastery)

By the 11th century AD, Buddhism had spread to the upper Himalayan regions of Tibet, Ladakh and Kashmir. Surrounded by high mountains, these areas developed their own unique aesthetics in an atmosphere of comparative insularity, excelling in metalcraft and wood carving, and using a synthesis of Buddhist and Brahmanical iconography.

The tradition of Buddhist architecture here was started by Rinchen Zangpo, a Tibetan monk, who is said to have initiated the construction of 108 monasteries and temples.

The *gompa* or monastery of this region was of two types. Tibetan Buddhism allowed some monks to stay in their village homes and gather in monasteries only at specific times of the year. These *gompa* were built near the villages and were usually small, nondescript groups of buildings clustered around a large central space.

Other monks had to meditate in solitude over long periods of time, having taken strict vows of asceticism and abstinence. They lived in large fortress-like *gompa* built on steep cliffs and mountain tops. These *gompa*, with heavy walls and battlements, reflected the power and influence of Buddhism at that time.

Monastery Design

Within the monastery was the *lhakhang* or temple, which consisted of at least two spaces, sometimes expressed as separate buildings. The *dukhang*, or core of the temple, was a large hall where the main deities were installed and where the monks assembled for prayer. The entrance of the *dukhang* always faced the east. The sacred texts were kept in the *dukhang*, either in the main hall or in smaller chambers opening off it. The *gonkhang* was the second space, a chamber reserved for meditation and ritual.

The interior walls and ceilings of both the *dukhang* and the *gonkhang* were covered with exquisitely colored murals, many of which were *mandala* or diagrammatic paintings governed by a strict geometry and iconographic code, and which served as meditational devices for the residing monks.

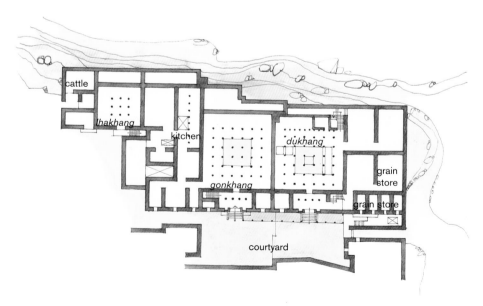

The *gompa* and *lhakhang* were enclosed by inward-sloping piled-up rock walls with mud plaster on both sides, sometimes covered with a lime wash. Square wooden windows slanted toward the interior to let in light. The windows were outlined on the exterior in black and maroon, black being the color to ward off evil spirits. The roofs were either flat or gabled, depending on the density of rainfall. Intricate wood carving was used to create ornately designed pillars, brackets and triangular pediment forms, especially in the interiors, which were then painted over in bright colors.

Most of the buildings were made of brick, including the flooring, with the size of brick being standard across all Buddhist monasteries.

The Chorten

The *chorten* evolved from the *stupa* but it is more often used as a votive object. Formal *chortens* are built to honor Buddhist saints or spiritual leaders. Many are simple structures; the more colorful ones depict the eight major events in the life of the Buddha. The Himalayan counterpart of the *torana* was the *kankani*, a freestanding gateway with two mud walls and a sloping slate roof. The *mane* (prayer stone) wall, unique to the upper Himalayas, was a low mud-plastered rubble wall used as a meditational device with a Buddhist *mantra* inscribed on it. A *chorten* is commonly found on travel routes, with prayer flags raised on it to ensure protection for the traveler.

Monastery walls are covered with paintings depicting mythological deities, legends and representations of the Buddha.

Left and above: A series of *chorten* usually indicates the vicinity of a temple or monastery. They contain the relics of saints or holy texts. Different levels of the *chorten* are symbolic of the five elements into which the human body merges upon death.

Sacred Hindu Architecture

The religious architecture of Hinduism, spanning more than a thousand years, consists of diverse temple forms, ranging from remote rock-cut temples to immense temple-cities. Although Hinduism has a complex and vast pantheon of deities, the Hindu temple is based on an essentially simple and direct concept of worship, with the ritual of prayer always directed towards a single deity.

The Hindu temple is built in the image of the created world, and laid out in accordance with elaborate symbolic graphic systems. In Hindu cosmology, the circle represents the earth, and the square the sky and cosmic order. The square is the governing form for the habitation of the gods, the temple.

Top left: Plan of a tower with seven *ratha*, external recesses and internal indentations on each side of the *garbha griha*.

Top right: Plan of a *pancharatha shikhara* with external recesses and internal indentations in the *garbha griha*.

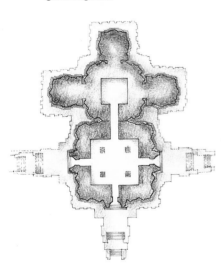

Above: Plan of the temple at Konarak.

Right: Devotees pray before a row of stone *linga*, the phallic symbol associated with the god Shiva.

Hindu worship is embodied in the concept of *darshan* or experiencing the divine. It is not congregational in nature but a private communication between the devotee and the god, with the priest acting as the intermediary.

Hindu gods and deities are essentially divine counterparts of humans, and are imbued with a combination of supernatural and human qualities and needs. The human qualities are manifested in the need to sleep, be awakened, bathed, clothed, fed, married, taken out in procession, and propitiated at given times of the day and year. The process of prayer includes rituals of cleansing, dance and music.

Hindu gods may display anger or vengeance if thwarted, and many of the rituals of worship,

consisting of offerings of flowers, incense, fruit, money, indeed anything deemed to be of value to the devotee, are also rituals of propitiation.

Deities and gods are worshipped in the form of an image or symbol enshrined in a temple, which is regarded as their home. It is here that all the rituals of prayer and sacrifice take place.

The Hindu Temple–Sanctum Sanctorum
A temple always houses one main deity to whom it is dedicated but it may also have a number of minor shrines dedicated to lesser gods, or to the consort of the main deity. The sanctum of the temple is a small chamber or cella with a decorated door frame, within which the image of the deity is installed. Known as the *garbha griha*

(literally "womb house"), it represents the microcosm of the universe and is always square in plan and elevated on a plinth. Its placement on the site coincides with the point of total harmony and equilibrium calculated according to the *Vaastu Purusha Mandala* (see p. 30). The image of the deity is placed in the exact center of the *garbha griha*, around which is an ambulatory passage. The cella and the passage together are called the *prasada*.

Other Parts of the Temple

Hindu cosmology supposes the earth to be a flat disk revolving around a pivot. The pivot represents stability, while the space beyond is chaos. Mount Kailasha, the abode of the gods, is the pivot around which the earth rotates. Expressed as the *shikhara* (mountain peak), or high towering roof over the sanctum, the apex of the *shikhara* is the highest point directly above the image to be worshipped. The heavens are represented on the exterior through bands of ornate sculpture with icons of gods and lesser beings associated with divine myths. The *shikhara* is topped with a finial, or *stupi*, which is installed at the consecration of the temple. Its form is a synthesis of various elements, including the *kalasha* or water urn.

Built in AD 500, the Vishnu Temple at Deogarh in central India is probably the earliest surviving example of the freestanding Hindu temple. The sandstone temple, now no longer containing its shrine image, consists of a 5-meter-square sanctum over which stands the *shikhara*, now very much damaged.

The *mandapa*, a hypostyle hall meant to shelter devotees and provide a space for some of the more public rituals, precedes the *garbha griha*. It is generally open on three sides, with ornate pillars supporting the roof, which is always much lower than the *shikhara*. A temple may have more than one *mandapa*, with separate functions allocated to each and named accordingly. A hall dedicated to dance is thus the *nat mandir*, while the hall for divine marriage ceremonies is the *kalyana mandapa*. The porch leading into the *mandapa* is called the *pragriva* or *ardha mandapa*, while the vestibule of the *garbha griha* is the *antarala*. The Hindu temple is planned strictly according to the *Vaastu Shastra*, and the *ardha mandapa*, *mandapa* and *garbha griha*, which are always axially aligned, are set within a compound which is surrounded by a colonnaded hall and sometimes encircled by smaller shrines. The compound is entered through a well-defined gateway or *gopuram*.

The presence of water, used in ritual cleansing as well as during consecration rites, is a necessity. Within the temple compound is usually a special tank or *kund*, containing water deemed to come from the sacred River Ganga.

Left: The lintel of the richly carved doorway of the Vishnu Temple is adorned with an image of the god Vishnu reclining on his coiled serpent. Each of the three exterior walls has a single niche containing sculpted panels with different images of Vishnu, the Preserver.

43

Hindu Rock-cut Temples

Stone image inside the Rani Gumpha cave temple at Udaygiri in Orissa.

The earliest surviving examples of Hindu temple architecture follow the style of Buddhist cave and rock-cut architecture which had, by the 4th century, developed into a fine architectural tradition. Continuing this tradition, early Hindu shrines incorporated many iconographic formulae based on the *Vaastu Shastra*.

There were two kinds of rock-cut architecture. The first was hollowed out of a steep cliff and comprised vast internal chambers. The other was carved into a freestanding rocky outcrop and may altogether lack internal spaces. The basic rock-cut temple consisted of a small chamber preceded by a rock-cut verandah. The doorway had decorated jambs and lintels, faithful copies of wooden prototypes. The entrance was usually guarded on either side by carved images of lesser deities or divine doorkeepers called *dvarapala*. Each temple was dedicated to one of the major gods: Shiva the Destroyer, Vishnu the Preserver, or the mother goddess, manifested as Durga or Kali.

The process of replicating the structural elements of wooden architecture in stone is indicative of the energy of the mason being concentrated in the creation of carvings rather than the structural exploration of the material.

The Kailashanatha Temple at Ellora

The Kailashanatha temple is an example of both cave and freestanding rock-cut architecture and is part of a complex of 34 caves at Ellora in the Deccan hills, of which 17 are Hindu shrines. A group of Buddhist caves already existed here. The later series was created largely under the patronage of the Rashtrakuta king Krishna I, who reigned from AD 757 to 783, and are fine examples of rock-cut architecture.

The Kailashanatha Temple, dedicated to Shiva, is the largest monolithic structure in the world. It shows the shift from stone-cut to stone-made architecture, with evidence of the use of both techniques. The cliffside of the hill was first excavated and the freestanding island of rock thus obtained was sculpted to create a complex that consists of a central monolithic temple and a series of caves hewn into the inner face of the excavation. The complex has three separate units: a gatehouse or *gopuram*; a pavilion to house Shiva's vehicle, the bull Nandi; and a cruciform temple with a pillared hall that leads to the central shrine which houses a massive stone *linga* (phallic emblem of Shiva). The temple is built in the Dravidian style, topped with a *stupi*-shaped finial. Life-size

King Kharavela of the Cheta dynasty, who ruled Kalinga, near Bhubaneswar in Orissa, in the 1st century BC, celebrated his conversion to Jainism by decreeing the excavation of a series of caves out of the surrounding hills. Many of these caves are still in an excellent state of preservation. The Rani Gumpha cave temple at Udaygiri (right) has two stories, all carved from rock, with arches supported by pillars that give the appearance of wooden architecture.

monolithic elephants flank the entrance to the complex, and it has two freestanding columns or *stambha*.

The exterior is covered with sculpture, as is the inside. Narrative friezes include the descent of the River Ganga, depicted here as a goddess, and an account of the demon king Ravana shaking Mount Kailasha, Shiva's mountain abode. The panels inside, which were probably stuccoed and painted over with vibrant colors, bear testimony to the considerable evolution of art and sculpture in ancient India.

The Udaygiri Caves

Although most of the cave temples at Udaygiri, in Orissa, are inspired by Jainism, two out of the twenty rock-cut chambers are Hindu temples, dating to the 4th century and created under Gupta patronage. The principal deity in these is Vishnu, depicted in one of his ten incarnations as Varaha, the boar. There are stone-cut images of a host of other deities as well. These include Ganesha, the elephant-headed son of Shiva; the goddess Durga in her form as the ten-armed demon slayer; and the holy rivers Ganga and Yamuna shown as goddesses guarding the entrance, one standing on a *makara* or crocodile, and the other on a *padma* or lotus.

The Badami Caves

The cave temples at Badami in the Deccan, dating back to the 6th century, are planned to a simple spatial definition. A simple verandah, supported by stone columns and brackets, serves as the entrance and leads into a *mandapa* interspersed with columns. The shrine housing the idol is much smaller than the *mandapa*, and is cut into the far end of the cave. It is square in plan and has a carved doorway. A distinctive feature of the Badami caves is their brackets, carved in the shape of figures, which became a major decorative motif of Deccan architecture.

The Elephanta Caves

The rock-cut temple in the caves of Elephanta, a small island 10 kilometers off the coast of Bombay, was built in the mid-6th century. The element of sculptured animal guardians, in this case elephants, is used effectively here. The cave measures 40 meters from north to south and has an elaborate plan, with side chapels cut into the rock around a massive courtyard-like space. The main temple has a large pillared *mandapa*, within which stands a freestanding square shrine surrounded by a circumambulatory passageway. At the four corners of the *mandapa* are images of Shiva in his many moods.

Top and above: Elevation and exterior view of the Kailashanatha Temple at Ellora. A gigantic monolithic rock was carved out of the hillside and then fashioned into a temple. In aspect it has all the aspects of a typical Dravidian temple, comprising a gateway (*gopuram*), a courtyard, a large hypostyle *mandapa* and an imposing tower (*shikhara*).

The Evolution of the Hindu Temple

Stone sculpture of Durga in the temple at Bhojpur.

Opposite below: Typical iconography depicting different aspects of gods and goddesses on a Hindu temple.

Stone Architecture

The transition from rock-cut to stone-made structural architecture, which marked a shift in emphasis rather than replacing one structural style by another, had begun by the 7th century. The temple, initially a simple shrine housing an image, soon evolved into an impressive edifice. Richly decorated with sculptures, the entire volume of the building was conceptualised as a sculptured complex of stone, rather than as a combination of support and canopy.

Rock-cut architecture was based on building into a stone mass, with the outward defining form being that of the cave itself. The act of building with and not into stone resulted in the creation of an autonomous building form which retained, however, the structural conservatism of cave architecture.

Stone temples continued to use the techniques of timber construction as their prototype, with enormous columns and beams, massive lintels and elaborate brackets replicating in faithful detail all the elements of the timber originals. Over the *garbha griha* was a superstructure of finely dressed blocks of stone placed pyramid-like one on top of the other without the use of mortar, although the support of iron beams was taken in the construction of the *shikhara*. (In the Dravidian or South Indian style, the sanctuary and the superstructure together are called the *vimana*, see p. 48.) The basic principles of pillar and lintel construction dictated that spaces were interspersed with columns, and most Hindu temples do not have a large clear space within. The *mandapa* was usually roofed with roughly hewn slabs of stone, placed on a structural network of stone beams. The jointing between beams, brackets, columns and stone blocks was done through sockets and dowels. Stone blocks were overlapped in successive courses to create the dome-like space within. The *shikhara*, massive and solid, had no windows or fenestrations. Lighting within the *garbha griha* was achieved through oil lamps, while the *mandapa* received natural light since it was open on three sides. The temple exteriors were richly embellished with complex sculptures and exquisite iconography.

The Ratha

The *ratha*, a replica of the main shrine, is a portable shrine mounted on a horse-drawn chariot. On certain preordained auspicious days in the year, the main deity of the temple is taken out in grand procession in a specially designed *ratha*. The *shikhara* of the *ratha* is usually made of bamboo and is covered with a finely embroidered cloth. This ritual of procession, in turn, influenced the concept of the temple to such an extent that the freestanding temple came to be known as the *vimana* or *ratha*, both words meaning "vehicle." Moreover, stone replicas of the chariot became a notable feature of many temple complexes.

The most famous example of the processional *ratha* are those taken out at the Rath Yatra of Lord Jagannath, incarnation of Vishnu, at the Jagannath Temple in Puri, Orissa.

The Ratha Yatra in Puri.

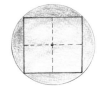

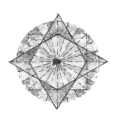

Left: The Kailashanatha Temple at Kanchipuram in Tamil Nadu, built in the 8th century by the Pallavas. Dedicated to Shiva, it is built in the tradition of temples that celebrate the cosmic mountain.

Below (top to bottom): Development of the ground plan of an ancillary shrine of the Brahmeshvara Temple at Bhubhaneshwar.

Iconography

Art and architecture were merged to conceive and define the Hindu temple. A certain set of norms, derived from the enormously complex vocabulary of Hindu iconography, formed the basis for the sculptural scheme of the temple.

Most Hindu temples are dedicated to Shiva the Destroyer, Vishnu the Preserver, or Shakti, Kali or Durga, aspects of the mother goddess. Brahma the Creator is rarely worshipped. In the whole of India, there are only three temples dedicated to Brahma. Iconographic symbols associated with each deity form the decorative lexicon of the temple. The principal deity, his or her consort and lesser gods are all assigned designated spaces within the temple precincts.

The sculptural imagery depicts a variety of beings: antigods or *asura*; guardians of the door or *dvarapala*; mythical beasts called *yali*; celestial nymphs or *apsara*; and guardians of the earth's treasure or *yakshi*. The water pot or *kalasha* is usually a part of the finial, as is the *amalaka* or fruit. The lotus or *padma* is used as a decorative element on ceilings.

Over time, the Hindu temple assumed its distinct forms and styles due to geographical and historical influences and varying interpretations of the *Vaastu Shastra* by successive royal patrons. The two main styles are broadly classi-fied as the Dravidian or South Indian style, and the Nagara or North Indian style of temple architecture.

47

The Dravidian Style

The Dravidian or Southern style is the earlier of the two main styles in the evolution of sacred Hindu architecture. It defines the prolific building activity of several South Indian ruling dynasties from the 7th century onwards, with each dynasty developing a distinctive style within this broad framework. It contains many stylistic elements which can be traced back to vernacular prototypes as well as to Buddhist origins.

Detail from the entrance *gopuram* of the Meenakshi Temple at Madurai.

A bird's eye view of the Nataraja Temple at Chidambaram, Tamil Nadu, believed to be the site of the god Shiva's cosmic dance.

The Temple Form

The most distinctive feature of the Dravidian style is the articulation of the *vimana*, a composite of the *garbha griha* and superstructure or spire (*shikhara*) which is a trapezoidal structure, starting on a square base, and soaring up in a series of well-articulated stories called *tala*. The *shikhara* represents the celestial abode. This is reinforced by the *kudu*, an arched apertural motif derived from the opening of the Buddhist *chaitya* hall and resembling in shape the leaf of the Bodhi Tree. Each *tala* is defined by a horizontal series of *kudu* that house gods and goddesses, creating the semblance of a divine mountain city with homes and occupants.

These components or aedicules grouped around the *shikhara* vary in number and in the degree of complexity with which they are integrated. The tops of the aedicules echo the roof shapes of earlier vernacular styles.

The *shikhara* is topped by a finial called the *stupi*, whose antecedents may be traced back to the *stupa*. In variations of this theme, the *shikhara* of the sanctuary has a wagon-vaulted roof, a replica of the original thatch, but carved out in stone. The ends of the vault are sculpturally defined by a variation of the *kudu*, and the roof has a series of finials along its length. The *shikhara* rests on walls made of dressed stone blocks with pilasters, or on pillars known as *pada*, again with distinctive capitals and shafts. The entablature is also a clear-cut feature, defined by carved moldings and other decorative embellishments.

The temple stands on a plinth known as the *adisthana*, which is defined by a series of horizontal bands. Later examples of the style show the division of the plinth into two distinct parts, the lower portion being called the *upapitha*.

Structure and Decoration

Temples were regarded as symbols of power. Built by kings, they were often added to by later royalty. The cumulative symbolism of power took the form of concentric shrines, with new gateways being added to the original shrine.

Earlier Dravidian temples were built entirely of stone. However, the building mass of the *shikhara* and the foundations which were required to support its weight were a structural challenge and a major source of expense. Hence, a shift took place whereby the temple, up to the entablature, was made of stone, and the *shikhara* was made of brick.

Decoration of the brick *shikhara* was done with terracotta sculpture, painted over with a special lime mixture of mineral colors.

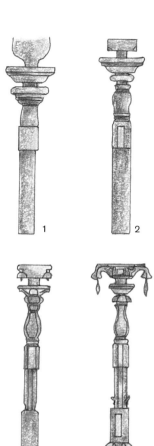

Evolution of the column from different periods of Dravidian architecture:
1 Pallava (7th–9th century)
2 Chola (10th–12th century)
3 Pandya (12th–13th century)
4 Madura Nayak (14th–18th century)

The temple tower of Sriranga-nathaswami Temple on Srirangam island in Tiruchirapalli, Tamil Nadu. It is said to be the tallest temple tower in India and is typically painted with the *panchavarnam* (five colors)–blue, red, green, yellow and black–which is seen on many Dravidian temples.

The Pancha Ratha at Mamallapuram

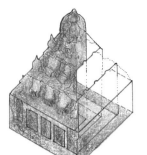

Above (top to bottom): Elevation, axonometric drawing and section of the Dharmaraja or Yudishthira Ratha, the largest of the *ratha*.

The Bhima Ratha, whose design is based on one of the fundamental forms of Indian architecture– the elongated meeting hall.

A Prototype for Temple Construction

The Pancha Ratha or Five Chariots at Mamallapuram in Tamil Nadu, South India, are a fine example of the evolution of form and the range of architectonic language in Hindu architecture.

Built in the 7th century AD by the Pallava dynasty, the Pancha Ratha are a group of monolithic shrines carved out of an outcrop of pink granite, with no discernible use but to serve as a prototype for actual temple construction. Named after the protagonists of the great epic, the *Mahabharata*—Draupadi, Arjuna, Bhima, Yudishthira, Nakula-Sahadeva—their composition is remarkable for its variety of plans and elevations.

Forms of the Pancha Ratha

The first *ratha*, called the Draupadi Ratha, is an almost exact replica of a palm-leaved thatched hut. It has carved relief statues of Hindu goddesses on either side of the simulated entrances. The stone entrances are faithful copies of wooden columns and beams.

The Arjuna Ratha, which has a two-tiered stepped pyramidical roof, shares its plinth with the Draupadi Ratha. The roof form of this *ratha* shows the use of the *kudu* motif (see p. 48), and of barrel-shaped housing forms, called *shala*, which were typical of a vernacular form. The roof is carved with several layers of *kudu* and crowned by a squat finial, representative of the mountain, but deriving its form from the Buddhist *stupa*. This is called the *stupi*. The high relief sculptures on the walls echo the wooden column and beam construction that must have been structural elements in the original.

The third *ratha*, called the Bhima Ratha, reproduces the concept of the *chaitya*, with a central hall, flanked along its length by a colonnaded corridor. The barrel-vaulted roof echoes on its exterior what the Buddhist *chaitya* halls of Ajanta sought to reproduce in their interiors. The Bhima Ratha is a replica of a meeting hall. The exterior of the roof again has the *kudu* motif carved all over it.

The Dharmaraja or Yudishthira Ratha,

the largest of the five *ratha*, is square in plan, and its three-tiered roof, capped with a stone finial, is ornamented with *kudu*. Its columns and the pilasters within the walls are carved with deities, again indicative of a wooden original.

The last *ratha*, the Nakula-Sahadeva Ratha, is a fairly faithful copy of the Buddhist *chaitya*, clearly showing its apsidal end. The rectangular building, decorated with *kudu*, and with the columns and beam-trabeated structural style replicated in relief on its walls, copies a wagon-vaulted structure made originally of wood.

The Shore Temple

Nearby the Rathas is the Shore Temple at Mammallapuram, built by Narisimhavarman II Rajasimha around AD 700, on a promontory that juts out into the ocean. Unlike the monolithic *rathas*, it is made of finely dressed blocks of local granite. Its slender tower rises 16 meters above the beach. Though its principal deity is Shiva, behind it is a secondary temple whose idol is Vishnu.

The **Shore Temple of Mammallapuram** differs from the customary plan and orientation of temples owing to its unusual site on the seafront. The cella was designed to face eastward so that the first rays of the morning sun would fall on the shrine, and it would be clearly seen by those approaching the harbor. The cella therefore touches the sea, leaving no room for a *mandapa* or even an entrance gateway.

The *rathas* of Mammallapuram. A stone Nandi (bull), the mount of Shiva, is built out of a single rock and faces the Arjuna Ratha. The *ratha* was in reality a chariot, provided by the temple authorities to carry the image of the deity during processions.

The Brihadishwara Temple at Thanjavur

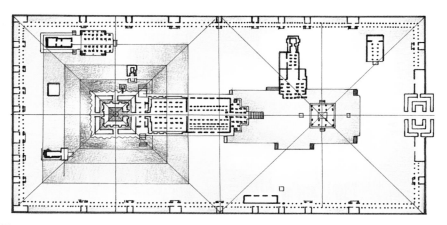

Plan and elevation of the temple.

Chalukyan Architecture
Under the Chalukya dynasty of central Deccan, established in the mid-5th century, a style of architecture developed that exhibited the continuity between Buddhist and Hindu architecture, and was a major influence on later kingdoms of the region. The Durga Temple at Aihole in Karnataka, built between AD 675 and 725, is a fine example of this style, combining Buddhist and Hindu elements in its planar and elevational articulation. The *garbha griha* is apsidal in plan, reminiscent of the Buddhist *chaitya* hall. The *mandapa* that precedes it continues around the apse, creating a covered gallery for circumambulation that is airy and well-lit because its external surface is actually a series of pillars resting on sturdy capitals which are exact copies of wooden columns. The entrance to the temple is through a vestibule, also axially aligned to the other elements. A small *kudu*-embellished *shikhara* is placed over the sanctum, and the rest of the temple is roofed with outwardly sloping stone slabs. The *shikhara* used to be topped by an *amalaka* finial, which has since fallen off.

The Main Temple
The foundations of the Brihadishwara Temple at Thanjavur were laid in AD 1002 by the Chola king Rajaraja I. Dedicated to Shiva, it is also known as the Rajarajeshwara Temple. Although constructed according to Chalukyan and Pallavan architectural principles, the scale of the main temple, as well as the grandeur of its sculpture, typify the Chola tradition.

A strict axial and symmetrical geometry governs the planning of the temple. A square *garbha griha*, within which is placed a massive stone *linga*, forms the focus. It is surrounded by a narrow corridor, axially aligned to which are two *mandapa*, separated from the main sanctuary by a four-columned vestibule or *antarala*. The *garbha griha* can be entered from the *mandapa* as well as from two impressive flights of steps that flank the *antarala*. The inner *mandapa* is a square hall enclosed by massive stone walls, whose interior space is broken by six bays of six columns each, creating a central bay axially aligned to the *garbha griha*. This *mandapa* leads out to a rectangular hypostyle *mandapa*, which in turn leads to a porch supported by twenty columns and accessible by three staircases. This again is preceded by a small open *mandapa* dedicated to Nandi, Shiva's sacred bull and mount. The Nandi *mandapa* shares with the main temple a stone plinth that leads up to the porch of the structure.

The Adjoining Structures
The main temple is surrounded by two walled enclosures. The inner enclosure consists of a portico defined by a wagon-vaulted *gopuram* with a double row of more than 400 pillars, and enclosed by a wall. A high wall defines the outer precinct of the temple, and is punctured by a *gopuram* more massive than the inner one, also axially aligned to the main temple.

The inner space of the *garbha griha* at its base measures only 5 meters square. However, the massive stone wall, within which lies the circumambulatory passage, reaches an outer measurement of 15 meters on each side, its dimensions obviously created to bear the weight of the immense stone *shikhara*, which rises to a height of nearly 70 meters. The *shikhara*

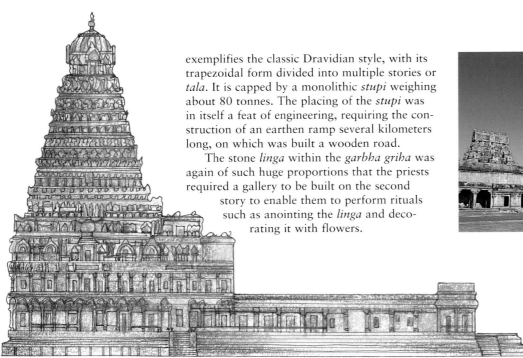

exemplifies the classic Dravidian style, with its trapezoidal form divided into multiple stories or *tala*. It is capped by a monolithic *stupi* weighing about 80 tonnes. The placing of the *stupi* was in itself a feat of engineering, requiring the construction of an earthen ramp several kilometers long, on which was built a wooden road.

The stone *linga* within the *garbha griha* was again of such huge proportions that the priests required a gallery to be built on the second story to enable them to perform rituals such as anointing the *linga* and decorating it with flowers.

The temple gateway of the Brihadishwara Temple.

Left and below: The impressive pyramidal *shikhara* of the Brihadishwara Temple. A domed monolithic *stupi* adorns the multistoried roof, which rises nearly 70 meters high.

Architecture of the Vijayanagara Dynasty

Sculpted relief of Shiva and Parvati from Hampi.

The shrine in the form of a stone *ratha* or chariot in front of the Vitthala Temple. The shrine honors Garuda, vehicle of Vishnu, to whom the entire temple is dedicated. The Vitthala Temple is considered the high point of Vijayanagara architecture.

The City of Victory

During the 14th to 16th century, the Vijayanagara kingdom of South India prospered away from the wave of Islamic domination that was sweeping over the north of the country at the time. It was founded by a prince who chose to establish his capital in the eminently defensible town of Hampi on the banks of the River Tungabhadra in Karnataka, surrounded by a landscape of granite boulders. Over 200 years, successive rulers expanded the city and filled it with magnificent specimens of sacred as well as secular architecture. They fortified it, dammed the river, carrying its waters through an aqueduct cut out of the solid rock, and transformed the barren landscape to a cultivable and splendid site.

Hampi contains a sacred center and a royal center (see p. 116). When the city finally fell to Islamic armies in 1565, the royal center became the focus of building activity of the conquerors, and much of the architecture that stands there today is Islamic. The sacred center, on the other hand, retains several temples of the earlier period that are an integral part of sacred Hindu architecture.

The dynasty reached the climax of its glory under the ruler Krishnadeva Raya (r. 1510–29)

with fabulous endowments being given to temples. Not very large in size and exhibiting a lightness in structure, these temples were distributed over the uneven terrain, the largest being the Vitthala Temple.

The Vitthala Temple

Adopting Narasimha, the mythical half-lion and half-man, as their emblem, the Vijayanagara kings used the granite locally available for their architecture. The virtuosity of the builders is best seen in the Vitthala Temple, dedicated to an incarnation or *avatar* of Vishnu.

The temple, commissioned by Krishnadeva Raya, who reigned between AD 1509 and 1530, has several features that distinguish the architecture of the dynasty. The main temple is the focus of an enclosed complex that contains within it several pavilions and *mandapa*. The *garbha griha* and its preceding *mandapa* form a single unit from the outside. The vast *ardhamandapa* that precedes these is axially aligned and rests on the same plinth. It is open on all sides, its roof resting on pillars that break up the expanse of the interior.

The pillars of the temple are a special feature. Monolithic structures, they consist of a base carved in the shape of four small squatting lions, on which rests the shaft. This is again carved to create a single central member with four surrounding colonnettes, each with its own base, shaft and capital, unified at the top by a single capital. The colonnettes are supposed to produce different musical notes when struck. The pillars, each carved from a single piece of granite, create a feeling of weightlessness that is further enhanced by the wide, overhanging eaves of the roof, which has at each corner a small upwardly sweeping claw-like embellishment. The pillars that flank the entrance steps on the sides of the *mandapa* are monolithic renderings of mythical beasts, astride which are warriors.

A stone chariot or *ratha* with granite wheels, dedicated to the mythical bird Garuda, Vishnu's mount, stands facing the *ardhamandapa*. The *shikhara* of the temple, as well as that of the surrounding *gopuram*, was probably constructed of brick. Both of these structures have long since been destroyed.

The Nayaks of Madurai

The story of South Indian temple architecture is not complete without mention of the Nayak kings, who ruled from Madurai, Kanchipuram and Thanjavur between AD 1334 and 1736. The Nayaks defended their kingdoms from Muslim invaders, and their architecture is associated with the development of the temple-city (see p. 50), which reached a dazzling climax under them. Here, a central temple was surrounded by successive walled precincts with gateways.

The Jambukeshwara Temple, built in the 17th century on Srirangam island in Tamil Nadu, exemplifies the exuberance of Nayak architecture. The main shrine, dedicated to Vishnu, is a small structure with a curved barrel-vaulted roof covered with gold. It forms the center of a series of five concentric precincts. An outstanding feature of the temple are the several freestanding *mandapa*, each supported on extravagantly decorated pillars with equally ornate painted ceilings.

The great *gopuram* of the Jambu-keshwara Temple. Some of these enormous structures went up fifteen stories high.

Below: The Vitthala Temple complex at Hampi. A series of restoration efforts have brought new life to its granite ruins.

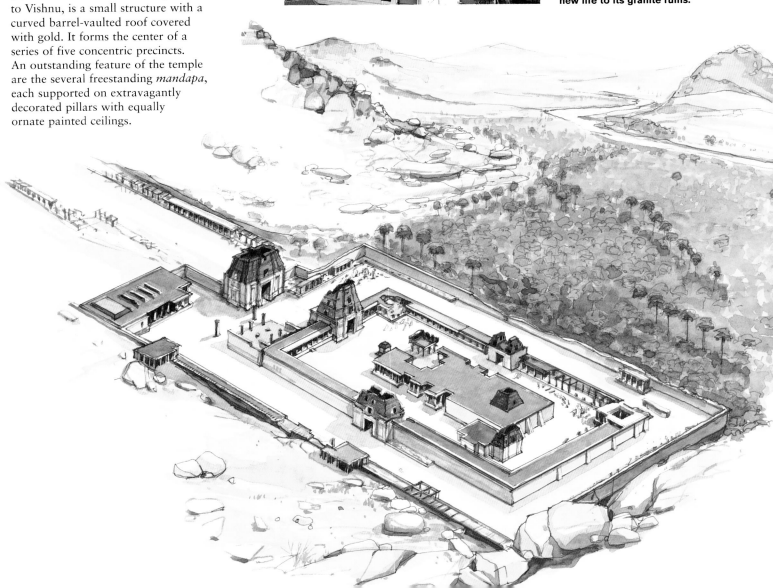

The Temples of Kerala

A narrow strip of land along the southwestern coast of India constitutes the region of Kerala. The tropical climate, heavy rainfall and fertile soil, in which over 600 varieties of trees grow, as well as early trade contact with East and Southeast Asia, and with the Phoenicians, Romans, Arabs, Chinese and Europeans, influenced the creation of a distinctive style of art and architecture in this region.

A temple in Trichur, Kerala. Composed of several individual buildings, including the main shrine, the roofs are covered with sloping tiers of terracotta tiles typical of the overhanging Kerala roof, sometimes broken by projecting eaves.

A characteristic of Kerala temples is that they consist of several separate buildings which achieve unity by being surrounded by a walled enclosure. The main shrine is known as the *srikovil*. A unique spatial feature of the *srikovil* is that it can be square, rectangular, circular or apsidal in shape. The apsidal shape traces its origins to Buddhist *chaitya* halls, and was probably introduced into the region through sea trade with South Asia. The temples were often built on stone basements; in fact, these basements are the only surviving elements in temples built prior to the 8th century. Abundant availability of wood resulted in the superstructure of later temples being made mainly of wood (if not in brick), covered with a tiled roof. A large number of these still survive intact, and there

are also some temples which are double-roofed. Wooden "sculpture" was generally preferred to stone. The Dravida tradition is evident in the external walls of some temples, which have rows of pilastered niches for elevations.

The *srikovil* is often enclosed by a rectangular cloister known as the *nalambalam*. The *mandapa* are detached from the main sanctuary. The main *mandapa* preceding the *srikovil* is called the *namaskara mandapa*. The temple complex also contains a hall known as the *kuttambalam*, for ritual theatrical and dance performances.

The Kerala Roof

Kerala temples are notable for their dramatic roof shapes. The heavy pitched roofs of these temples can give the impression of Chinese

Far Eastern Influence

Another strong regional form emerging not only as a response to climatic conditions but also influenced by contact with the Far East over Himalayan travel routes, is that of the temples of the northern mountain region. These temples are located in areas that are snow-bound for large parts of the year, and where the diversity of building material includes slate, timber, mud and rubble. Local vernacular traditions of building that resulted from these two factors are used as the basis for construction.

Pitched roofs topped by a finial and tiled with slate, resembling the pagoda of the Far East, rest over walls, the lower part of which may be made of mud bricks, wattle and daub or even dressed stone. The upper part of the walls is made of wood. The easy availability of wood has also resulted in a well-developed tradition of wood carving in the Himalayan temple. The building on the left is the palace-cum-temple complex of Bhimkali, dating to the 7th century.

architecture. This, together with the fact that Kerala had trade contacts with China, has led some scholars to suggest a Chinese influence on its art and architecture. A likelier explanation is that these roof forms evolved as a response to the heavy rainfall of the region.

The roof is often multistoried, diminishing in area and height as it rises, an arrangement that serves to emphasise the overall height and to create a feeling of lightness. Even when it is single-storied, the smooth uninterrupted expanse of the roof, covered with overlapping clay tiles or sometimes with metal sheets, contrasts with the richly embellished walls that support it. As in temples in other parts of the country, a finial forms the apex of the roof. Another distinctive characteristic of the roof is the manner in which it projects well beyond the walls, thus serving as a protection for the painted murals and wood carvings on the walls.

A special feature of Kerala temples is the use of wood as a major structural element. Legends abound of Kerala's master carpenter, Perunthachhan, and the exuberance and perfection of his craft is evident in the intricate carvings found on pillars, brackets and ceilings in many temples of the region.

The Vadakkunnathan Temple at Trichur in central Kerala, one of whose buildings has a double roof. The Pooram festival, at which there is a procession of bedecked elephants, takes place here annually.

The Subramanya Temple at Payyanur, an example of the Kerala temple in apsidal form.

The interior of a *kuttambalam*, with its wooden ceiling specially designed for good acoustics. The hall is surrounded by wooden pillars and *jaalis* on three sides to provide ventilation.

The Nagara Style

The Nagara, or the North Indian style of sacred Hindu architecture, which developed after the Dravidian style, is exemplified in the temples of Madhya Pradesh in central India, Orissa along the east coast, and some parts of western India, including Rajasthan and Gujarat. The distinguishing characteristics of this style are the shape of the *shikhara*, the roof of the *mandapa* and the plan of the *garbha griha*.

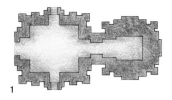

Above: (1) Typical plan of a temple. (2, 3, 4) The development of the *mandapa* in a series of Hindu temples in Bhubaneshwar: hypostyle pavilions of the 8th, 9th and 12th centuries. The last is a corbeled roof comprising a succession of *pidha*.

Characteristics of the Nagara Style

The interior plan of a Nagara shrine is always square, but the exterior is defined by a series of extensions which, as they increase in number, may transform the plan till it becomes cruciform in shape. Based on the complex *mandala* of the *Vaastu Shastra*, the projections alter only the outer face of the sanctuary, giving the entire superstructure a distinctive form.

The *shikhara*, standing over a cubical *garbha griha*, is distinguished by its convex curvilinear profile. The planar projections occurring on the walls of the cella continue along the height of the *shikhara*, emphasising the analogy of the mountain peak. In many examples, a clear division into stories, defined by horizontal bands of carving, can also be seen. The main *shikhara* may have a series of projecting aedicules around its root, which are smaller replicas of its own profile. The surface of the *shikhara* is generally covered with fine carvings. The *shikhara* is crowned with a finial, whose most distinctive component is the fluted disk-shaped *amalaka*, representing the *amala*, a fruit which has medicinal qualities.

The *mandapa*, especially in the later examples of the Nagara style, also have a distinctive trapezoidal roof, lower than the *shikhara*, which is characterised by successive horizontal bands, topped again by an *amalaka*-shaped finial.

The characteristic Nagara temple stands on a plinth adorned with elaborately profiled and rhythmical horizontal moldings.

Within the broad defining characteristics of the Nagara style, there are clear-cut distinctions between the temples of Orissa and those of central India, best seen as at Khajuraho.

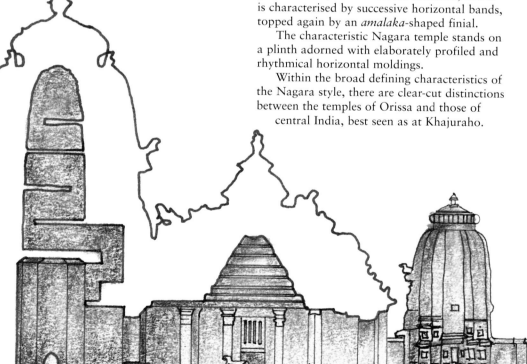

The Temples of Orissa

Although traces of Buddhist architectural forms are discernible, for example, in the roof form of the temples of Orissa, the addition of several original elements endows them with a unique quality. The outer surfaces of the vault are largely unadorned. Specific names are given to every part of the temple. The shrine and super-structure of the temple (*shikhara*) is called a *deul*, while the *mandapa* is called a *jagmohan*. The main type of *deul* form is the *rekha deul*, characterised by the curvilinear shape of the *shikhara*. Another, rarer form, the *vaitul deul*, is wagon-vaulted in shape. The trapezoidal roof over the *jagmohan* is known as the *pidha*, a term referring to its characteristic horizontal platforms or bands.

The *deul* and the *jagmohan* consist of four vertical units, based on parts of the human body, moving upward from the ground.

The plinth is called the *pista*, and corresponds to the feet. Though distinctly defined by horizontal moldings, it does not project out.

Then comes the *bada* or wall, corresponding to the legs. The *bada*, with imitative pilasters, is covered with bands of sculpted freizes alternating with carved motifs.

The next unit, the *gandi* or trunk, refers to the curvilinear *shikhara* of the *deul*. A distinctive feature of the *gandi* is the series of projections at each of the four corners that divide it into horizontal levels, or *bhumi*. Each *bhumi* is demarcated by a ribbed *amalaka*.

The head, or *mastaka*, the uppermost unit, includes all the elements of the finial, the main ones being the *amalaka* and the water urn or *kalasha*. Crowning them all is the *ayudha*, which is the emblem of the deity to whom the temple is dedicated. It is usually a trident for Shiva temples and a disk for Vishnu temples.

The Sun Temple at Konarak

An Architectural Masterpiece

The magnificent Sun Temple at Konarak, 60 kilometers from Bhubaneshwar in Orissa, was commissioned by King Narasimha I of the Ganga dynasty, who ruled from AD 1238 to 1264. Also known as the Black Pagoda, the construction of this architectural masterpiece took as many as sixteen years to complete and engaged the services of many thousands of workmen. The temple is dedicated to Surya, the sun god, a cultic deity since Vedic times, worshipped by followers of Shiva and Vishnu alike.

Deriving its concept from the *ratha* or chariot, the Sun Temple was probably built at the site of an earlier temple. It was conceived in design as a colossal processional chariot of the god with twelve pairs of massive, intricately carved wheels, and drawn by seven sculpted horses in galloping motion across the horizon. The seven horses symbolise the days of the week, and the twelve wheels represent the months of the year.

Structure of the Sun Temple

The main temple consists of two main structures, the sanctum or *deul*, which houses the image of the deity, and the assembly hall or *jagmohan* which precedes it. Both the structures were built over a high platform, around which are the wheels and horses seemingly pulling the great mass of the temple along. The structure of the sanctum now no longer stands, with little remaining of it except for the platform, from which an idea of the original structure can be derived. The *shikhara* or the *deul* probably rose to a height of over 60 meters, and was built in the classic Nagara style of Orissa. It is believed to have collapsed because it was too heavy for the weak soil, being so close to the sea.

The walls of the sanctum had deep niches on three sides, each containing a larger-than-life statue of Surya, the sun god, unique in the Hindu pantheon because he is shown wearing boots of leather, a substance considered polluting to Hindus. The images were placed so that each one, in turn, caught the rays of the sun at sunrise, noon and sunset.

The *jagmohan*, which is the best-preserved building in the complex, is a cube-shaped structure with a three-tiered pyramidical roof rising to a height of 30 meters. The internal space was vast, one of the largest internal spaces in Hindu architecture at about 20 meters square. The three diminishing tiers of the roof pyramid consist of separate and horizontally developed bands, or *pidha*. The recesses between them have been enlarged into wide terraces, where life-size, freestanding sculptures of temple dancers and musicians, some of the most powerful in Indian art, have been placed at regular intervals. The *jagmohan* was built over thick stone walls and additionally supported by four massive central piers, spanned by stone lintels reinforced with wrought iron, but in spite of this support, the roof was perceived to be structurally unstable.

Above: The entire base of the Sun Temple represents a processional chariot drawn by seven sculpted horses. The smallest details of hub and spokes are reproduced on the luxuriously carved wheels of the chariot.

Right: A colossal statue of Surya, the sun god, to whom the temple is dedicated, sculpted in gray-green metamorphic stone.

Detail from the Sun Temple.

It was once punctured on three sides by beautifully proportioned doorways but these are now walled up and the inner space reinforced.

Axially aligned to the *jagmohan* but separated from it by a flight of steps is the dance pavilion or *nat mandir*, also called the *bhog mandir* because this is where offerings were made to the gods. The pavilion is no longer roofed, but the pillars that supported what was probably a flat stone slab roof are still intact, and are covered with carvings and friezes of dancers and musicians.

A pair of gigantic stone lions flanks the flight of stairs that leads up to the *nat mandir*, each rearing over a crouching elephant. The longer sides of the terrace on which the temple has been built are sculptured with reliefs of twelve massive wheels, each more than 3 meters in diameter, and are one of the most noteworthy features of the Sun Temple. Each wheel has sixteen spokes and is a faithful stone replica of the wooden original, down to the minutest detail of hub and axle pin. The wheels are ornately carved and depict various deities and rich floral motifs. *Kudu* motifs, celestial figures and couples eternally frozen in erotic poses of love-play cover the sides of the platform, in a hierarchized pattern of horizontal friezes.

The entire temple is made of yellow-colored stone, and the images of Surya, made of gray-green chlorite, form a striking contrast.

Above: Detail on a carved wheel.

Below: Of the vast original complex of one of the greatest of all Hindu temples, only the *jagmohan* has survived almost intact. Konarak is supposedly the first attempt at sculpting freestanding statuary on a temple.

The Nagara Style of Central India

Right: The Devi Jagdamba Temple at Khajuraho, dedicated first to Vishnu and then to Kali, stands on the same plinth as the Kandariya Mahadev Temple. They are built of fine-grained buff, pink and pale yellow sandstone.

Opposite: Intricate sculpted friezes run around the projections of the outer wall of the Devi Jagadamba Temple.

The Vishwanath Temple. As in all the other Khajuraho temples, the external rippling effect is achieved by the projecting and receding sculpting of the walls.

The Central Indian Temple Plan

A complex cruciform plan with a series of re-entrants is one of the features of the Nagara temples of central India. A special spatial characteristic of these temples is the manner in which the elements of *vimana*, *antarala*, *ardhamandapa* and *mandapa* blend harmoniously in a single building, with each element retaining its own distinct identity.

In elevation, the temple consists of three distinct zones. The lowest part of the temple is a high platform-like plinth with a series of distinct horizontal moldings, known as the *jagati*. Over this rises the wall or *bada*, providing ample surfaces to create a series of extremely ornate sculptural decorations. The *shikhara*, which is the third main zone, is again distinct in that the corners rise beyond the central portion so that they accentuate the verticality of the whole structure. Another important distinguishing feature is

the finial which consists of not one but two *amalaka*, the higher, smaller one bearing the *kalasha*. In the *mandapa*, balconied windows puncture the upper part of the wall of the temple. Projecting out between the horizontal bands of carved ornamentation, these windows create a contrast of light and shade on the exterior as well as the interior of the temple.

Khajuraho

Of the 85 temples originally built at Khajuraho, the capital of the Chandela kings who ruled over central India between AD 916 and 1203, 25 still stand, as testimony to the exquisite architecture of the Nagara style of central India. Built between AD 1025 and 1050 by King Vidyadhara of the Chandela dynasty, the magnificent Kandariya Mahadeo Temple, dedicated to

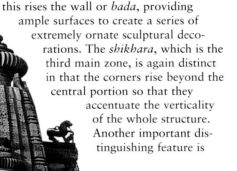

Shiva, represents the culmination of the Nagara style. Two other temples, the Devi Jagadamba and the Mahadeva, share the 4-meter-high plinth of the seven-projection temple.

The cruciform temple, aligned on the east–west axis, is 22 meters long and 12.5 meters wide. Its *shikhara* rises to a height of 32 meters above the level of the plinth. The *mandapa*, *garbha griha* and ambulatory corridor form a single flowing space lit by the *ardhamandapa* and five verandahs. The *garbha griha* measures 2.5 by 3 meters and contains a *linga*. Every interior unit has its own pyramidal roof, each loftier than the earlier one.

The profile of the temple is reminiscent of the rising peaks of a mountain range, culminating in the main *shikhara*. This incorporates a cluster of 84 smaller towers, with the sharp projections and deep recesses creating a dazzling interplay of light and shade. The surface of the *shikhara* is covered with fine carving, the main decorative feature being a miniature replica of the *shikhara* itself. Over 600 sculptures dominate the exterior architectural form. Divine beings and amorous couples in various poses are carved in high relief. The interior of the temple contains over 200 sculptures depicting Hindu iconography.

Erotic Iconography

Hindu temples have long been a source of wonder to those who do not comprehend fully the many manifestations of worship in Hinduism that are an integral part of experiencing the divine presence. An aspect that has given rise to many interpretations is the presence of erotic sculpture and iconography that, in varying degrees, are an essential part of the embellishment of the temple, always on the outer walls. Hinduism, with its roots in the later Vedic religion, adopted and synthesised into its mainstream many pre-Aryan beliefs and practices. These included fertility rites and worship of the mother goddess. As the pastoral Aryans settled down to become village agriculturalists, fertility came to be a cherished attribute of every important god. It was expressed in the concept of *mithuna* or sexual love, and its expression was accepted to be as natural a presence as sublime or celestial love. Links between fertility, sexuality and the auspicious are thus strong in Hindu society. The erotic iconography found in Nagara temples, like that at Khajuraho, is a tribute not only to the architectural perfection of the temple and the superlative skills of the Indian sculptor. It also celebrates the human aspect of deities and thus, the power of love and the perpetuation of life, expressed in all its manifestations.

Solanki Architecture

The Lati-Nagara Style

The Solankis were a prosperous dynasty that ruled over western India from the latter half of the 10th century till the end of the 13th century. Based on the Nagara style, Solanki architecture displays a complexity of plan and temple form, an increase in decoration and a stylisation of figural sculpture that merit it being classified as a subtype known as Lati. The Sun Temple at Modhera is a highpoint of this style.

Keeping intact the spatial arrangement of a square *garbha griha* preceded by an axially aligned *mandapa*, Solanki architects experimented with the placement of pillars as well as the outward shape of the shrine to achieve a vigorous aesthetic that translated into a complementary complexity of form. The most outstanding aspect of this concept was the manner in which the re-entrants and projections around the basic square shape were carried upward elevationally, to create a cascade of smaller *shikhara* clustered around the main *shikhara*. The roof of the *mandapa* was pyramidical in style, but rather than being a single pyramid with horizontal platforms, it was made up of a complex cluster of small pyramids which rose upward in a defined order of ascent.

The Lati style is distinguished by the manner in which interior spaces are treated. The dome of the *mandapa* rests on an octagonal arrangement of pillars, thus leaving open a large central space which creates the sense of a pavilion rather than an enclosed room. The dome itself is the result of a finely crafted system of corbeling. The stone beams that make up the corbels ascend in a series of concentric circles. The roundness of the interior is achieved because of the large number of projections.

While the Dravidian or South Indian temple is rich in outward embellishments, with relatively stark interiors, the concentration of sculptural adornment in the Nagara or North Indian temple is on the outside. The Lati temple displays an equal degree of sculptural luxuriance on the exterior and interior. The fine carving is a product of the long-standing tradition of stone carving in Gujarat, which served as a model for the stone equivalent.

Detail from the Modhera Sun Temple, renowned for its elaborate stone carvings, most exquisitely done on a freestanding stone *torana*, which stands between the tank and the temple.

The temple at Somnath represents the scale, planning and elaborate nature of the Solanki style of architecture. It was built in the 10th century on the Arabian Sea coast of India, and was one of the twelve most sacred shrines dedicated to Shiva. Because of its vulnerable location and wealth, it was plundered and destroyed several times. The present stone temple was almost entirely built anew in 1950.

Left and above: The Modhera Sun Temple is dedicated to Surya, the sun god. Built during the reign of Bhima I (AD 1022–63), the main temple consists of three distinct elements. The porch, known as the *sabha mandapa*, is an open cruciform pillared hall, axially aligned to the rest of the temple but separate from it. Next comes the assembly hall, called the *gudha mandapa*, and finally the *garbha griha*, with its surrounding circumambulatory passage. The *sabha mandapa*, which has four entrances, is preceded by a huge tank, called the *kund*. The tank of the Modhera Temple is one of the largest in all of South Asia.

Hoysala Architecture

Synthesis of Dravidian and Nagara Styles

The Hoysalas ruled over an independent southern kingdom in what is Karnataka today, beween AD 1110 and 1327. They came to power after a long struggle with the Cholas of the south, and partly because of their hostility to their adversaries, partly because, like the Chalukyas, they had a stronger affinity with the north, they did not wholeheartedly adopt the Chola style. Originally followers of Jainism, the Hoysalas later turned to Hinduism and built many opulent temples.

The temples of the Hoysala dynasty are a landmark in the development of Hindu architecture because they exhibit a synthesis of the Dravidian and Nagara styles, creating a distinct hybrid one, sometimes called the Vesara style.

Hoysala temples were built on a highly original stellar or star-shaped plan—which developed as a result of more than one central *garba griha* or inner cella—with a series of re-entrants and projections. This concept was based on the square as the primary form which, as it was rotated around a fixed center, produced a number of intersecting projections resulting in a star shape. The concept was refined over time, and later, the basic stellar plan was developed to create a high platform that runs around the entire temple and projects outward to form an open terrace for circumambulation. This terrace, with its continuous horizontal moldings, also allows the intricate sculptures that cover the walls of the temple to be viewed by devotees and visitors from close quarters.

Influenced by the temples of Khajuraho, the Hoysala temple was conceptualised as an organic whole, and various spatial elements such as the *mandapa*, *ardhamandapa* and *vimana* were merged to create a unified and cohesive space.

Construction of the Temples

The Hoysalas used dark steatite stone in the construction of their temples. This material, being softer than the granite used elsewhere, lent itself to the intricate carving that is a defining characteristic of this architecture. Another defining feature is the use of lathe-turned columns, with moldings based on wooden counterparts. These columns, with their shafts looking like a stack of disks, were sometimes further carved with deep flutings that followed the changing outline created by the lathe. The use of panels of stone latticework between pillars to create a visual screen, is a further marker of this style of architecture.

Among the outstanding works of the Hoysalas is the Chennakeshava Temple at Belur (AD 1117), followed by the Hoysaleshwara Temple at Halebid (AD 1150), culminating in the Keshava Temple at Somnathpur (AD 1268).

The plan of the Hoysaleshwara Temple shows the developing complexity of the stellar form. The complex comprises twin temples built on a common platform, and rigorously symmetrical in plan. The only asymmetrical elements are the two pavilions that precede the temple, dedicated to Nandi, the sacred bull.

Sculptural Virtuosity

The sculpture in Hoysala temples is a reminder of the virtuosity of the craftsmen as well as of the superb planning that integrated this essentially decorative feature with structural elements. The star-shaped plan with its series of re-entrants provided the sculptor with an extended canvas. The ceiling, essentially still following the method of placing stone beams diagonally across a square space to create a dome-like interior, was covered with an intricate pattern of ornamentation. The exterior of the temple is embellished with geometric, floral and animal motifs, as well as narrative friezes depicting scenes from various Indian epics. Many of these friezes bear the sculptors' names, and are probably the first instance of signed works of art in India.

Above: The Chennakeshava Temple at Belur, dedicated to Vishnu.

Left: The double cruciform plan of the Chennakeshava Temple shows the beginning of the stellar form that was a hallmark of Hoysala architecture. The stone *shikhara* was demolished long ago, and only the supporting masonry structure remains. The *nat mandapa* or dance hall that precedes the *garbha griha* is a hypostyle hall with three entrances at three cardinal points. The fourth cardinal point gives access to the sanctum, which is a tiny square cella lying on the central axis, and preceded by an *antarala* or vestibule of the same size.

The Terracotta Temples of Bengal

Early engraving of the Dakshine-shwar Temple on the east bank of the Hooghly River. Built by a rich and pious widow in 1855, it is one of Bengal's most popular monuments. It stands in a large compound which includes twelve smaller temples, bustling with activity. The main temple, painted in white, is set on a high plinth and topped with nine cupolas offset by the typical *bangaldar* roof. The temple is dedicated to the goddess Kali, whose image is placed inside the sanctuary.

An Offshoot of Vernacular Traditions

The terracotta temples of Bengal are examples of a unique form that developed in medieval Bengal that combines vernacular building traditions with elements of the Nagara temples of Orissa. These temples, though confined to the clay-rich area of the Bengal delta, stylistically influenced the architecture of other regions.

The earliest examples date back to the mid-17th century. They were built mostly from clay, though there are some examples of laterite construction. The clay, found in abundance in the area, was either molded into bricks which were then kiln-fired, or shaped into panels which were used as a decorative element.

The temple stood on a low but distinct brick platform. The platform also served as an open ambulatory passage around the building. The plan of the temple was usually square. Thick brick walls rose on all four sides, and arched entrances punctured the walls of the temples, sometimes on all four sides. The openings were supported on massive brick pillars, richly carved on all sides with ornate architraves. Well-defined pilasters and lintels served to break the surface of the walls, which were covered with intricate decorations in relief. Some of the terracotta relief panels had elaborate patterns, either geometric or ornamental. These were interspersed with larger panels showing episodes from the epics or scenes from everyday life.

The roof, also made of clay, was the defining element of the temple form. Reflecting vernacular traditions, the roofs can be classified into two main types—*chala* and *ratna*. Stylistically derived from the architecture of the thatched hut of Bengal, the *chala* is also known as the *bangla* or *bangaldar* roof. The *chala* may slope on either two or on all four sides. A variation of the *chala* has the main roof split into twin roofs, both with a two-sided slope. This is known as the *jor bangla* style.

The Keshta Raya Temple

Built in AD 1655 by the Malla king Raghunatha Singha, the Keshta Raya Temple is dedicated to Krishna, one of the ten *avatars* of Vishnu. It rests on an almost square platform measuring nearly 12 meters on each side, and rises to a height of nearly 11 meters. Its main entrance is from the south, through a three-arched aperture with thick, intricately decorated pillars.

It is formed of two hut-type structures, with two-sided sloping roofs that join together in the middle, which is why it is referred to as the *jor bangla* (twin roofs). The front of the temple has a triple-arched entrance. On top of the main roof, coincidental in plan with the sanctum, is a square tower with a four-sided sloping roof, over which rests a small brick finial. The canvas of the walls is broken by semi-octagonal pilasters which rise to the full height of the temple, decorated with figures of dancers.

Rich decorations in terracotta grace the exterior façades of the temple. These are a combination of geometric and floral patterns as well as intricately carved relief panels showing scenes from the life of the god Krishna. However, the interior of the temple, by contrast, is stark, with plain, unadorned walls.

In temples of the *ratna* style, the main structure has a two-sided sloping roof, atop which is a *shikhara*-type tower. Where there is only one tower or *ratna*, it is always placed over the space occupied by the idol. The single-towered temple is of the *ek* (one) *ratna* style. Temples may also have five (*pancha ratna*) or nine (*nava ratna*) towers, with the central tower flanked by lower ones. The towers are spire-shaped, with faceted sides and defined horizontal ribs, reminiscent of the stepped pyramidal roofs of the Nagara *pidha*. Each spire is topped by an *amalaka*. Except for the roof, all the other elements of the *ratna* style of temples are similar to the *chala* type.

The Shyama Raya Temple

Built by Raghunatha Singha in AD 1643, the Shyama Raya Temple is of the *pancha ratna* style. Built entirely of brick, the temple is square in plan. It measures 11.4 meters on each side and rises to a height of nearly 11 meters. The temple stands on a low brick platform that extends on all sides, and its side walls are broken by three-arched entrance porches which are decorated with elaborate tilework. The dark inner sanctum is accessed by a long corridor, which also leads to four corner chambers.

The roof of the Shyama Raya curves on all four sides and is formed in several layers. Over each corner is a tower with a peaked roof, and from the center a taller single tower emerges, also with a pyramidal roof. There are thus five towers in all, the ones on the sides being shorter than the central tower. The spire of each of the towers is slightly different, though they are all topped with two *amalaka*.

The entire temple, including the walls, the pillars supporting the entrance arches, the walls of the tower and the spires, is covered with fine terracotta relief decoration, as is the interior. The main entrance bears an inscription that states that the temple is dedicated to the god Krishna and his consort Radhika. The tilework decorations depict various episodes and scenes from the life of Krishna as child, lover and god, as well as battle scenes and episodes from the *Puranas*, hunting and boating images, and other scenes from the everyday life of the times.

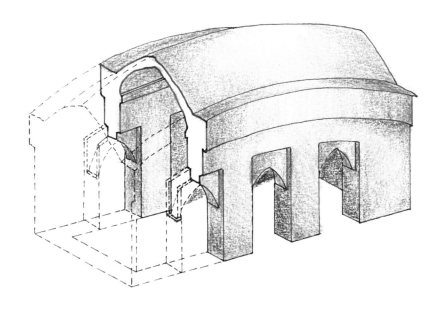

Above: Drawing showing the placement of the *bangaldar* roof, which slopes from a central point to either side, where it is held up by thick walls.

Left: The Keshta Raya Temple, an example of the *jor bangla* style of roof. Although the exterior form of this twin roof differs from the simple *bangaldar* roof, the interior of both is similar in plan. The sanctuary of the Keshta Raya Temple is a 3-meter-square cell surrounded by side chambers, from one of which a staircase leads to an upper gallery.

Opposite: The Shyama Raya Temple. Three sanctums are arranged in a cross on a sixteen-pointed stellate terrace. Thirty-three columns support the roof of the *mandapa*, while the three *shikhara*, which are still intact, rest on massive stone walls, which again are covered by a profusion of sculpture.

Sacred Jain Architecture

Jainism was founded in India by Mahavira, about the same time as Buddhism. For many centuries, Jain art and architecture was barely distinguishable from the dominant Hindu art and architecture of the times. Based on the same principles of planning as Hindu shrines, Jain temples followed the same pattern of evolution, progressing from rock-cut architecture to freestanding monuments.

Top: The feet of Mahavira Jain, a symbol of worship.

Above: Statue of Adinatha, the first in the line of 24 Jain *tirthankaras*, in meditation.

Right: Entrance gateway to the Jain temples at Lodurva near Jaiselmer. Architecture and sculpture complement each other superbly through intricately carved pillars and capitals and sinuous brackets that serve as strong supports.

Rigidly following the religious tenets of non-violence, Jain communities concentrated on professions of banking, trade and commerce. By the 11th century, they had prospered enormously, and their architecture, reflecting their wealth, began to achieve its own distinct expression. Hindu temples were primarily built out of materials such as granite, quartzite or other stone, locally available. To the affluent Jains, however, expensive materials were of little consequence and the 11th-century Jain temples mark the beginning of the use of marble, which was transported, often across long distances, to the building site. The texture and grain of this material lent themselves to exquisite and intricate carving. Jain builders combined the plasticity of marble with a finely developed tradition of wood carving, to create buildings that are sculpted on every inch of their surface, inside and out. The iconography mainly features the life and teachings of Mahavira, combined with Hindu iconography and decorative motifs. Mahavira was the last of the 24 teachers, known as *tirthankaras*, of Jain philosophy, and probably the only historical figure.

Architectural Elements

The plan of the Jain temple is almost identical to that of the Hindu temple of the Nagara style. It consists of a relatively small square shrine,

axially preceded by a *mandapa*. The two units, which form one unified space, are surrounded by a walled complex lined with small cells. Each of these cells usually contains an image of a *tirthankara*.

Following the Nagara style, the shrine is topped by a *shikhara* which dictates the form of the temple, and at its base is a cluster of smaller *shikhara*. As Jain architecture developed, each *tirthankara* had smaller *shikhara* positioned over them, so that the Jain temple came to resemble a whole mountain range, as opposed to the attempt of the Hindu temple to replicate only Mount Kailasha.

Another feature of the Jain temple is the emphasis on pillars, used in the *mandapa* to create a sense of space and lightness. They support a particularly interesting style of the serpentine bracket, as seen in Lodurva in Rajasthan, which creates the form of an arch and is a special feature of the Jain temple.

Following the Solanki tradition, Jain temples used the system of placing stone slabs on the pillars in an octagonal manner, creating dome-like interior spaces, again richly carved.

Jain temples reached a peak of perfection in the temples of Ranakpur and Palitana in western India.

The vast Jain temple complex at Palitana, in Gujarat, is situated on the upper levels of a mountain, and comprises more than 836 sanctuaries and shrines. The construction of this complex was begun in the 11th century, but it had to be totally reconstructed in the 16th and 17th centuries after the entire city was destroyed by Muslim invaders. The architectural forms here conform to the general outlines of the Nagara style, and are similar to those in other Jain temples at Mount Abu and Nagda.

The Jain Temples of Mount Abu

A detail from the ceiling of the Luna Vasahi Temple. Sixteen celestial nymphs form part of the delicate carving on the false dome of the temple.

The isolated site of Mount Abu, in the Aravalli hills of southern Rajasthan, has been one of the main pilgrimage sites for Jain devotees from the 11th century. The most spectacular examples of Jain sacred architecture are to be found here, a reflection of the expanding nature of the Jain religion. The complex of four temples at Mount Abu, which are similar in plan, are celebrated for the quality of the sculpture in them.

The Vimala Vasahi Temple, the earliest of the four temples at Mount Abu, was commissioned by the Solanki king Bhima I's minister, Vimala Shah, and completed in AD 1031. Legend has it that the temple was constructed as atonement for the sin of murder that the minister had to commit while carrying out the duties of statecraft. The Vimala Vasahi Temple is dedicated to Adinatha, the first *tirthankara*.

There is a statue of Vimala Shah seated on an elephant in a pavilion to the right of the entrance. The arches, pillars and the splendid eleven-tiered domed ceiling in the main hall are all adorned with nymphs, musicians, horses and elephants. The inner sanctum has a statue of Adinatha sitting in peaceful meditation. There are 52 carved niches containing images of the other Jain *tirthankaras*.

The Luna Vasahi, another temple dedicated to Adinatha, and the Parshvanatha are the other three temples in the complex. The first three temples are each contained within high walls lined with cells. The Parshvanatha Temple, which has a cruciform plan with several re-entrants, is without such a boundary wall.

The Luna Vasahi Temple dates to 1231 and is dedicated to Neminath, the 22nd Jain *tirthankara*. It is even more elaborately carved than the Vimala Vasahi Temple. Its most outstanding feature is its main hall, which has a lotus-shaped tiered pendant carved from a single block of marble descending from the domed ceiling. The Hall of Donors is situated behind the main shrine and contains life-sized statues of the donors and their wives.

The Luna Vasahi or Neminath Temple has a false dome profusely decorated. The dome rests on an octagonal base and is supported by pillars and false arches reinforced by brackets— a structural element used with superb mastery by Jain architects.

74

Above and left: The entrance to the Vimala Vasahi Temple also has a false dome which rests on finely carved serpentine brackets, akin to garlands. This technique of triangulated supports was the counterpart of the familiar technique of the decorative arch, which appears for the first time in this temple. The dome leads into an octagonal *mandapa*, whose pillars support a space achieved by corbeling. All the lintels are connected, arch-like, with similar triangulated supports reinforced by brackets.

Sacred Islamic Architecture

While Hindu architecture continued to evolve and flourish, political events occurred in the north of India in the 10th century that had huge ramifications in the development of the architecture and aesthetics of the Indian subcontinent. The political chaos that resulted from dynastic rivalries among ruling powers laid the ground for the forces of Islam to enter the country through mountain passes in the northwest.

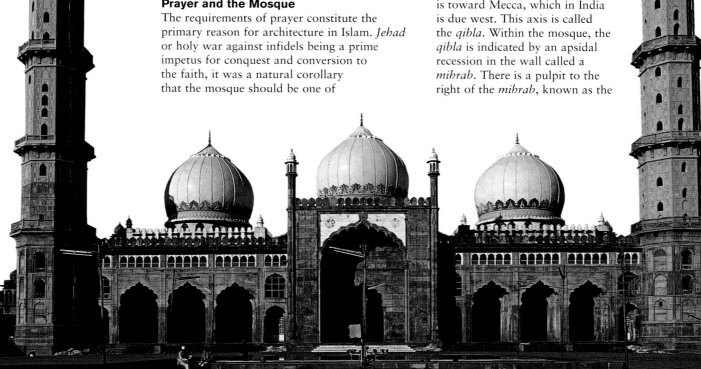

Above: Eid festival prayers at the Jama Masjid, Ahmedabad.

Below: Started in 1878, the Taj-ul Masjid, Bhopal, was completed in 1971. The complex is flanked by two 18-storied minarets.

The first of the Islamic forces to invade the subcontinent were the Ghaznavids of Afghanistan, led by Mahmud of Ghazni, who entered through the Khyber Pass. A series of expeditions with the twofold purpose of spreading Islam and accessing the country's wealth culminated in upsetting the political equilibrium of northern India. Mahmud of Ghazni finally retired, but another general, Mohammad Ghori, pressed into India. He left his slave-general Qutb-din Aibak behind to establish the first Muslim dynasty of India, the Mamluk or Slave dynasty. Aibak established his capital in Delhi, giving the impetus for a relationship between Hinduism and Islam that was to result in rich and hybrid artistic expressions. While it was for the Muslims to dictate the reasons for building, the act of construction was entrusted to the Hindu craftsmen of the conquered territory.

Prayer and the Mosque

The requirements of prayer constitute the primary reason for architecture in Islam. *Jehad* or holy war against infidels being a prime impetus for conquest and conversion to the faith, it was a natural corollary that the mosque should be one of the first building types to be built. The Koran prescribes a specific and precise ritual for individual and congregational prayer. While individual prayer may be done in private, congregational prayer, especially at noon on Friday (known as the *juma*), is carried out in the mosque or *masjid*, the sacred space for prayer.

The first mosques were built not only on the sites of vandalised temples (prime targets for destruction) but with material from the razed places of worship. They were places to congregate and did not adhere to any treatise or tradition of building. The only rule they observed was that laid down in the Koran—that there should be no human image or human representation of God.

The orientation of the believer is toward Mecca, which in India is due west. This axis is called the *qibla*. Within the mosque, the *qibla* is indicated by an apsidal recession in the wall called a *mihrab*. There is a pulpit to the right of the *mihrab*, known as the *mimbar*. The Koran is placed here, on a lectern, and passages are read out from this by the *imam* or priest as he leads the congregation.

The *muezzin* indicates the time for prayer by calling out from a high tower. This tower is known as the *minar*, and the mosque usually has a *minar* in each of its four corners. The large central domed chamber containing the *mihrab* is known as the *qubba*, and its evolution of form can be traced back to part-Roman, part-Parthian antecedents. A congregational hall, other than the *qubba*, often forms a part of the mosque and is called the *liwan*. The court of the mosque also contains a tank for ablutions.

Death and the Tomb

Islam requires that the dead be buried, the body being laid flat with the face turned toward Mecca. Followers of Islam believe that for all acts carried out in this life, they are answerable before Allah on the Day of Judgement. The tomb or *maqbara* was erected to contain the grave, and although not a place of worship,

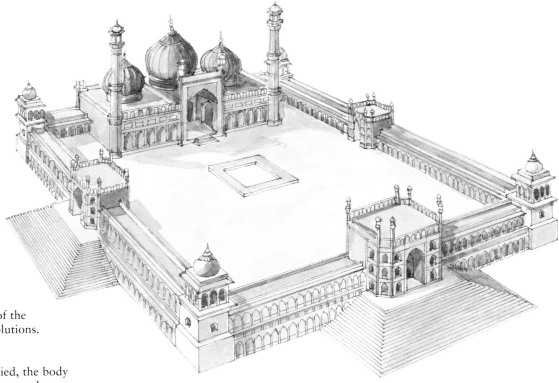

An overhead view of a typical Indian mosque. The literal meaning of the word mosque or *masjid* is "place of prostration." It consists of a rectangular courtyard called a *sehn*, with a tank used for ablutions at its center. A pillared cloister with many entrances, the *liwan*, surrounds this courtyard. At the western end of the courtyard is a domed prayer hall, which in India facilitates worshippers to face Mecca at the time of prayer. The back wall of the prayer hall contains a niche, the *mihrab*, to indicate the *qibla* or direction for prayer. To the right is a *mimbar*, the pulpit from where the *imam* conducts the prayers. The prayer halls of the congregational mosques, the *jami masjids*, often have a screened-off section for women.

is an intrinsic part of sacred architecture.

The grave or *qubr* is defined at the ground level by a cenotaph or *zarih* which rests on a raised platform inscribed with the 99 names of Allah and enclosed within a vaulted chamber, with enough space within for its occupant to rise when called to judgement. This chamber or *hujra* is covered by a dome known as the *gumbad* and constitutes the basic *maqbara*. Another tradition decrees that the chamber be marked by a series of freestanding arches, but that the actual grave be left open to the sky. Both traditions, however, believe that the demarcated space defines the orbit of benign influence or *barakat*.

This concept of *barakat*, or a microcosm of paradise, was further defined by placing the tomb in the midst of a special garden called the *chahar* or *charbagh*, literally a garden divided into four quadrants, with a defined central axis leading up to the tomb. Most Indo-Islamic tombs are therefore called garden tombs.

Tombs of saints are also called *zariat*, and form the core of important places of pilgrimage, or *dargah*.

The Five Pillars of Islam

Islam believes in Allah, the One God. The religion was codified by Muhammad the Prophet—the Chosen One—in the 7th century. The tenets of the faith are spelt out in the holy book, the Koran, which is considered to be the supreme revelation, dictated to Muhammad. Islam seeks to represent Allah not through imagery but through the passages of the Koran, which also contains the conditions for submission (or *islam*). The believer, or *muslim*, has certain moral obligations in the fulfillment of his faith. These are called the five pillars on which the Islamic faith rests, and are defined as the affirmation of the creed, prayer, fasting, alms-giving and pilgrimage, the highest level of which is the Haj to Mecca.

The Evolution of Islamic Styles

Islamic architecture can be broadly divided into three styles, which are defined by the historical events and the succession of Muslim ruling dynasties that shaped the destiny of India. Five successive Mughal emperors took a significant interest in architecture: Babur, Humayun, Akbar, Jahangir and Shah Jahan. While following a broadly chronological structure, there is sometimes an overlapping of styles.

Although sacred architecture in the form of the mosque and the mausoleum dominated the vast sweep of Islamic architecture, it was not without its secular counterparts, typified by the *madrassa* (school for religious learning), the *mahal* (palace), gardens and pavilions and the *qila* (fort).

The earliest phase of Islamic architecture in India is marked by the Sultanate style. Starting from the 12th century AD till the early 16th century, it encompasses the architectural activities of five dynasties (see p. 80), all of whom ruled from Delhi. The Sultanate was a distinctive style, following an established set of rules.

The second style of Islamic architecture is known as the Provincial style. It is based on the architecture of various kingdoms under Islamic rule in parts of the country other than Delhi. Each provincial kingdom had its own distinguishing features, which were the result not only of the geographical distance from Delhi but also of the degree of artistic influence and proficiency

The evolution of the dome (top to bottom): Sultanate, Mughal, Indo-Islamic.

Gol Gumbaz, Bijapur. Started in AD 1656, the tomb of Sultan Mohammed is a monumental example of the dome as an Islamic architectural feature. It transcends all other buildings in Bijapur with its sheer volume and mass. It is a square hall enclosed by four walls, buttressed by octagonal towers in the corner and surmounted by a hemispherical dome. With its diameter of 44 meters, this dome is the largest in the world.

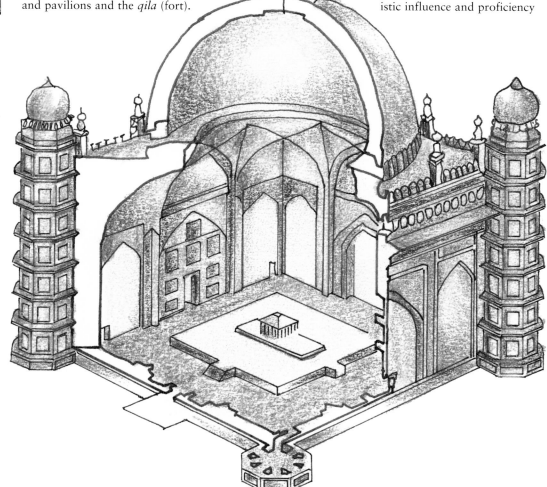

of the indigenous building activity of that region. Another significant influence on the Provincial style was the fact that foreign craftsmen were sometimes employed. One of the most important Provincial styles was the Gujarat style, a typical example of which is the Jami Masjid at Champaner, near Ahmedabad.

The third style of Islamic architecture, known as the Mughal style, refers to the extraordinary architectural activities of one dynasty, the Mughals, which was established in AD 1526. The Mughals ruled from Delhi, and were responsible for the creation of some of the most beautiful buildings in the world. The Mughal period can be broadly distinguished by the two major stones used for construction: sandstone, usually red, and white marble, as exemplified by the buildings of Shah Jahan.

The Dome and the Arch

The mosque and the tomb were introduced into India from the rich and well-developed architectural tradition of Western Asia. It is important to remember that both sacred and secular Islamic architecture share the same architectural forms. Thus, mosques and tombs, palaces and forts were all based on two dominant elements: the vault and the dome, resting on load-bearing masonry walls bonded with mortar; and the true arch, ranging in shape from the basic semicircular arch to the pointed ogee arch, the horseshoe arch and the cusped arch. (The true arch in India was first used in a screen of stone to emphasise the courtyard of the Quwwat-ul-Islam Mosque in Delhi built by Qutb-din Aibak, the first Muslim ruler.)

Existing Hindu, Buddhist and Jain traditions had created similar forms by using the technique of corbeling, while relying on the basically trabeate form of support with columns and beams. However, these methods of structural articulation had been petrified in the development and experiment of engineering techniques. The introduction into India of an already developed structural style led in a new, vigorous methodology of construction, while again displaying a degree of synthesis and cross influences. This synthesis was naturally articulated in explorations of spatial expression.

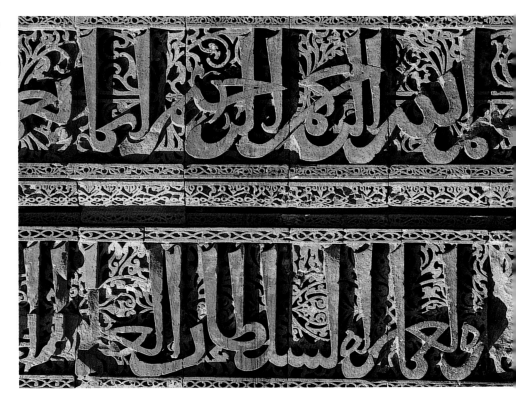

Islamic Art

Islamic art engages its viewer at an abstract level. Whereas Hinduism, Buddhism and Jainism seek to create sensuous and sumptuous images of their gods and deities, Islam uses the vocabulary of calligraphy, geometry and arabesques. This reluctance to represent a living form, especially the human form, was the result of an interpretation of one of the holy texts. It was believed that on the Day of Judgement, Allah would call upon the person who had created an image of a living being and ask him to breathe life into it. On being unable to do so, that person would be cast into the deepest hell for eternity.

This interpretation led to the belief that the representation of any living being was blasphemy, and hence the zeal for destroying the arts of those cultures that created such representations. However, the process of synthesis of cross-cultural influences that had existed in India for so many centuries continued under Muslim rule. Islamic calligraphic and geometric art blended with the Hindu, Buddhist and Jain art of representation of nature and man-made objects to create a rich decorative style.

The Sultanate Style

The systematic dismantling of existing temples and shrines, and reusing the stone to build mosques and tombs, marks the beginning of architectural activity under Islamic rule in India. This gesture was not only one of symbolic religious supremacy but was also based on the sound economic principle of saving costs. The realistic sculptural iconography and decoration that embellished the temples was disguised, usually by the simple expedient of defacing the human forms. Later, when economic consolidation and religious supremacy had been established, new material was especially quarried.

Muslim architecture in India was given a glorious start by the first of the five dynasties that come under the Sultanate tradition. These are: the Slave or Mamluk dynasty, who ruled from AD 1192 to 1287; the Khalji dynasty, whose reign lasted from AD 1290 to 1316; the Tughlaq dynasty, who ruled from AD 1320 to 1414; followed by the Sayyid dynasty, who ruled from AD 1414 to 1451; and finally, the Lodi dynasty, who ruled from AD 1451 to 1526. All five dynasties ruled from Delhi and the region is where their building activities were undertaken.

The first buildings constructed by each of the successive Sultanate dynasties utilised stone, acquired by dismantling a number of Hindu and Jain shrines in the neighborhood. This process of reuse, where the earlier sculpture was easily identifiable, soon became a distinguishing feature of early Sultanate architecture.

Hindu builders, who were sculptors and masons together, were responsible for the construction of these buildings, under the supervision of Muslim overseers and architects. The age-old techniques of construction that they were familiar with were adapted to the new architectonic language that they were introduced to, and the result was an architecturally hybrid style that began its process of evolution right from the earliest examples. By the time Hindu masons had become familiar with the new structural techniques imported from Central Asia, the synthesis of Hindu and Islamic architecture was firmly entrenched in the architectural vocabulary of the subcontinent. Thus we see the predominantly arcuate form being executed through the method of corbeling in the early examples of Sultanate architecture.

Top: Detail of an arch in the Jami Masjid of Sikander Lodi in Lodi Gardens, Delhi.

Above: Tomb of Mubarak Lodi, Delhi. Built in AD 1424, it has an octagonal base and a dome that is 9 meters high. There are merlons along the parapet and kiosks along the verandahs. The layout is more organised than the Tughlaq prototype.

Right: Section through Feroze Shah Kotla, Delhi, the palace complex of Ferozabad, the fifth of Delhi's famous seven cities. Feroze Shah Tughlaq was a prolific builder, credited with the construction of 40 mosques, 200 towns, 100 public baths and 30 reservoirs during his 37-year reign. This ruined site now contains a roofless mosque and the pyramidal structure shown here in which Feroze installed an Asokan pillar brought by him from the Punjab in 1356.

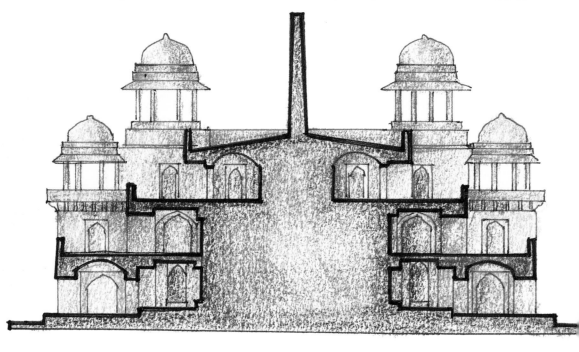

Architectural Elements

The original Islamic dome did not have a finial, an element that was an integral and important part of the Hindu *shikhara* and the Buddhist *stupa*. Indo-Islamic architecture adopted not only the concept of the finial, but also the motifs that defined it, and the Indo-Islamic dome is distinguished by the various ways in which these motifs have been integrated with the apex.

The walls, either straight or sloping vertically inward, as in the Tughlaq style, were solid, with the apertures being defined by the arch, giving the architecture of this dynasty its characteristic feeling of unyielding heaviness. Small niches, either in bas or high relief, sometimes eased the otherwise characteristic austerity and solidity of the façades, which were often decorated, in a comparatively restrained manner, with calligraphic carving in relief and the occasional floral motif. Later examples of Sultanate architecture, however, incorporated the arched façade built across the entire front of the mosque or sanctuary. This screen was a massive stone wall with openings and marked the beginning of an aesthetic that relied on beauty of proportion and a feeling of lightness for its aesthetic grace.

Later examples of the Sultanate style, especially the tombs of the Lodi kings, also saw the shift from the square plan to the octagonal. Projecting eaves and a part of the existing architectural vocabulary were incorporated along with smaller *chhattri* or domed cupolas around the basic dome, so that the relatively austere lines of early Sultanate architecture acquired a more extravagant outline.

The new materials were either quartzite stone masonry blocks, used with mortar or red sandstone. The sandstone was usually inlaid with black or white marble and blue schist. Some examples also show the use of relief work in stucco. The synthesis of Hindu and Islamic elements became total and complete by the time the last Lodi king had commissioned his tomb.

Decorative Elements

The Islamic vocabulary of architectural decoration relied on the use of calligraphy and geometry and the *jaali* or latticed screen. Earlier examples display carving into the stone itself as contrasted with the later, more sumptuous style of the Mughals who used the technique of inlay with black or white marble or semiprecious stones. The craftsmen of the early Muslim period, however, also adopted certain figural motifs commonly used by their predecessors, notably the lotus, which appear along with verses from the Koran engraved in stone in the Arabic and Kufic scripts. Even in the Quwwat-ul-Islam Mosque, which is the first example of Islamic architecture in India, decorative Hindu panels salvaged from razed temples around the site are juxtaposed with Koranic inscriptions.

Tomb of Ghiyas-ud-din Tughlaq, founder of the Tughlaq dynasty, in Delhi. Built in AD 1325, it is set in an irregular pentagonal fortified enclosure. Built outside the fortress city of Tughlaqabad, the third of Delhi's early capitals, the tomb houses the graves of both Ghiyas-ud-din and his son Muhammad. Constructed in red sandstone and inlaid with white marble, it is connected to the fortress by a 229-meter-long causeway that may have once been covered by water, but is now dry land.

The Mughal Style

The establishment of the Mughal dynasty in AD 1526 by Babur, descendant of the Timurid Mongols, was the start of one of the most prolific and dynamic phases of architecture in India. The buildings of the Mughal style form a robust and homogeneous group. The credit for this goes mainly to the first five of the Mughal emperors—Babur, Humayun, Akbar, Jahangir and Shah Jahan.

Babur supervising the construction of a reservoir near Kabul. Painting from the *Babur Nama*, (Babur's autobiography), National Museum, New Delhi.

Babur

With a small but well-organised army, Babur marched to Delhi from neighboring Afghanistan and defeated the Sultan of Delhi, Ibrahim Lodi, at the battle of Panipat. He established his capital in Agra, but his stormy reign lasted only four years. Babur did not leave any direct impact on building and, in fact, his memoirs display some contempt for the existing state of architecture in India, but his concept of the pleasure garden became an important landscaping element for later architecture.

The Mughal Garden

The Mughal garden was embodied in Babur's dream of trying to recreate the lush landscape of his native Ferghana. He found India harsh, hot and stifling, and the gardens that he laid out had fragrant flowers and huge trees, and the ever-present element of water, both in channels as well as fountains, so that the sound of it flowing

was reminiscent of his homeland. The gardens themselves were laid out according to a strict regular and geometric plan of quadrants, an earthly representation of paradise, with the emperor's place at the center, following the concept of the *charbagh* (see p. 77). The best examples of Babur's efforts indeed evoke visions of paradise, being named Bagh-i-Hast Bihist or Garden of the Eight Heavens at Agra and the Bagh-i-Nilufer or Lotus Garden in Dholpur.

Humayun

Babur's eldest son Humayun succeeded him to the throne in 1530. Though courageous and well read, he lacked his father's military skills and ten years and several campaigns later, lost his kingdom to the Afghan rebel noble, Sher Shah Suri of Bihar, and fled to Persia.

Sher Shah, however, ruled for only five years. He died of burns in 1545. Incessant strife during his son Islam Shah's five-year rule gave

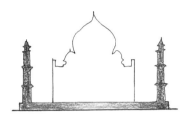

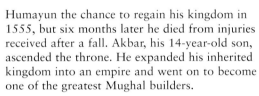

Humayun the chance to regain his kingdom in 1555, but six months later he died from injuries received after a fall. Akbar, his 14-year-old son, ascended the throne. He expanded his inherited kingdom into an empire and went on to become one of the greatest Mughal builders.

Humayun's Tomb

The tomb of Humayun marks the real architectural beginning of the Mughal style, characterised by a remarkable refinement of spatial symmetry and a classic attention to detailing. Humayun's tomb was built by his senior widow Haji Begum and took nearly nine years to complete. It is surrounded by a formal garden that retains its original layout and landscaping elements. Paved pathways divide the garden into four quadrants, with water channels, cisterns and basins crossing them at regular intervals. A high rubble wall encloses the garden. The tomb rests on a huge square platform 7.5 meters high and 99 meters on each side. This podium is made of red sandstone, with the façade containing a row of arched niches ornamented with white marble. On this rests the tomb itself, also made of white marble, measuring 47.5 meters square and 38 meters high till the top of the dome. Within the square is an octagonal chamber buttressed by four octagonal towers. On the central chamber rests a bulbous dome.

The dome is faced with white marble and has a double skin with a gap between the inner

and outer layers, an innovation that was to become a characteristic of some of the best examples of Mughal architecture, such as the Taj Mahal (see pp. 90–5). All fenestrations contain fine stone latticework screens or *jaali*. The four corner towers are crowned with domed *chattri*, which are the only discernible Hindu elements in an otherwise Persian building. First seen in the tomb of Humayun, the elegant proportions are an outstanding feature of Mughal architecture.

Akbar

Humayun's son Akbar is considered the greatest of the Mughal emperors not only because of the successful expansion of his empire but also because of his policies of secularism and his patronage of art and music.

Through a series of alliances with the Hindu Rajput kings against whom he had led military campaigns, Akbar succeeded in both consolidating and stabilising his empire. His kingdom spanned north India and no king could challenge him. He was thus the first Mughal king with the means and the opportunity to build extensively. He also created a new religious philosophy called the Din-e-Elahi, the tenets of which are remarkable for their tolerance of all religions. The most spectacular of Akbar's architectural endeavors, Fatehpur Sikri, the City of Victory, is a tribute to this ideology and is an avowedly secular agglomeration of royal buildings, which will be dealt with later in the book (pp. 118–19).

Above left: Sher Shah Suri's tomb at Sasaram. The pyramidal sandstone structure rises in five tiers in the middle of a man-made lake. On a high plinth stands the octagonal tomb, tapering elegantly toward the dome in three layers of arches, tiny pillared pavilions and parapets.

Above (top to bottom): Drawings showing the evolution of the monumental tomb.

Opposite below: Humayun's Tomb in Delhi, said to have been built under the supervision of Mirak Mirza Ghiyas, a Persian architect who had worked extensively in Herat and Bukhara. Commissioned by Haji Begum who was greatly taken by the Persian style of architecture, he gave India its first dome in the Persian tradition. Although purely Persian in style, it drew upon Indian elements such as the red sandstone and white marble which was a common feature of the architecture of the Delhi sultanate.

The Tomb of Itimad-ud-Daulah (Lord Treasurer of the Empire), considered to be the second most beautiful building in Agra after the Taj Mahal, was built by Empress Nur Jahan between 1622 and 1625 for her father, Mirza Ghiyath Beg, who was appointed the prime minister shortly after her marriage to Jahangir.

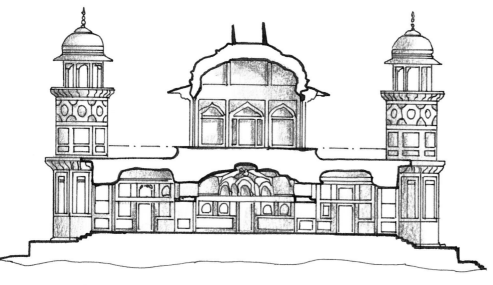

Above and right: Section and plan of Itmad-ud-Daulah's Tomb in Agra, built as a memorial to Itmad-ud-Daulah, father of Empress Nur Jahan, wife of Emperor Jahangir. Extremely graceful and feminine in plan, it is a building of modest proportions, with a plan some 21 meters square and a central structure enclosed within four octagonal minarets. A small pavilion on the summit is covered by a *bangaldar* roof.

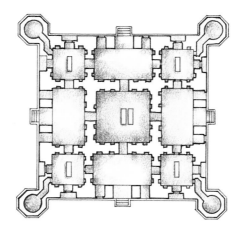

The Jami Masjid and Dargah of Salim Chisti at Fatehpur Sikri

Fatehpur Sikri's Jami Masjid stands on a high plinth constructed to provide a level surface on rocky terrain. The plinth is supported by arches and measures 165 by 133 meters. Made of the red sandstone that characterises almost all of Akbar's architecture, the mosque is enclosed within a courtyard or *sahn* that is almost the same size as the plinth. On two sides the courtyard walls consist of pillared porches which support wide cusped arch openings. They are surmounted by a wide *chhajja*, and the parapet is distinguished by a series of *chattri*.

The prayer hall, measuring 88 meters by 20 meters, is divided into three sections, the central section covered by a dome and flanked by two smaller cupolas. Within the hall is a splendid *mihrab* marking the *qibla*, embellished with engraved and painted inscriptions from the Koran. The main *mihrab* is flanked by two smaller ones, thus retaining a strict symmetry. All the arches, including the arch of the *mihrab*, have borders of lotus buds.

The entrance to the mosque is through a magnificent gateway, known as the Buland Darwaza. Built to commemorate Akbar's victory over Gujarat, this is a 41-meter-high structure built on a 13-meter-high stepped platform.

Within the courtyard of the mosque is the small but exquisite little tomb built in honor of the Sufi saint, Shaikh Salim Chisti, who rightly predicted that Akbar would have three sons when the emperor visited him for his blessings. In 1569, one of Akbar's Rajput queens, who later came to be called Maryam Zamani, or Mary of the Age, gave birth to his first son who was named Salim after the saint. The tomb is now a *dargah* or place of pilgrimage.

Salim Chisti's tomb is square in plan, each side measuring 14.5 meters. The entrance is to the south. Four slender pillars with very unusual struts that curve upward to the roof define it. The tomb is built entirely of white marble and provides a striking contrast to the surrounding red sandstone buildings. The main hall contains the sarcophagus of the saint, which is enclosed within an ebony structure inlaid with mother-of-pearl. Around the tomb chamber is a spacious verandah resting on pillars linked to each other with finely carved marble *jaalis*. A wide *chajja* runs around the entire building, supported on snake corbels with an extremely fine *jaali* infill (where pilgrims tie threads to invoke the saint's blessings). Verses from the Koran, selected for their special significance to the Sufis, are inscribed in relief around the outer walls of the tomb chamber.

Jahangir

Akbar's son Salim or Jahangir (Conqueror of the World) was a more enthusiastic patron of the fine arts than architecture. Akbar's mausoleum at Sikandra, outside Agra, is his most important work, though even about this, it is doubtful how much of the monument can actually be ascribed to Jahangir. Certainly it is true that the plan for his own tomb had already been drawn up by the eclectic Akbar who visualised a Buddhist stepped-up form of masonry over his subterranean grave. The more consciously Islamic elements, however, are Jahangir's contribution. Apart from the entrance minarets, which Shah Jahan built, these include the huge arched openings, the massive entrance gateway or certainly the white marble mosaic covering it, and the uppermost pavilion of delicately latticed marble, incongruous with the rest of the somber monument. With Jahangir, the era of marble had begun, to be perfected by Shah Jahan, who made building his passion.

The mausoleum of Akbar at Sikandra was Jahangir's most important architectural project. Like Humayun's mausoleum, it is also situated at the center of a *charbagh*. Surrounded by a perimeter wall, it has four portals. The southern portal constitutes the main entrance, while the others have false doors and were added for the sole purpose of providing symmetry to the whole. There is a fine mosaic of white marble and colored stone on the red sandstone of the building, forming intricate geometric and floral patterns.

The Taj Mahal

The most magnificent of all of Shah Jahan's buildings is the Taj Mahal at Agra in Uttar Pradesh, begun in 1631 and completed 22 years later in 1653, a tomb built in memory of his favorite queen, Mumtaz Mahal. The identity of the architect is disputed: some claim him to be an Italian, others say he was an Iranian, while still others claim that it was the emperor Shah Jahan himself. Constructed entirely of the purest white marble from Makrana in Rajasthan, the Taj Mahal is stylistically evolved from the tomb of Humayun in Delhi, but the refinement of the proportions, the breathtaking detailing and the flawless execution all combine to make it the finest building of the Mughal era. The Taj Mahal stands in a landscaped Mughal garden, flanked by two identical buildings in sandstone that effectively enhance its pristine marble.

Persian Prototypes

Mumtaz Mahal was originally buried at Burhanpur on the River Tapti where she died in childbirth at 39. Her body was transferred six months later to the present site of the Taj Mahal, personally selected by Shah Jahan. Fired with a passion to build a monument that would surpass all others in the world, he consulted books and architects for almost two years before finalising the design of the mausoleum. Shah Jahan himself no doubt played a major role in influencing the final outcome.

Some historians have endeavored to prove that the Taj Mahal was a purely Hindu monument. The grouping of the four small kiosks around the large false dome is credited by them to the Hindu *pancharatna* (five jewels) temple plan. The monumentality of the building also harks back to the Hindu idea of massiveness in architecture as expressed in monolithic towers or symbols of the cosmic mountain, Kailasha. However, few can disagree that Humayun's tomb is almost certainly derived from Persian prototypes. The exceptionally high dome of the Taj also recalls Persian monuments. Prototypes of the Taj Mahal start, in fact, with mosques in Damascus, Samarkand, and end with Khan Khanum's tomb, a small mausoleum in Delhi, which dates to a period in between Humayun's tomb and the Taj Mahal.

Top and bottom right: Elevation of the building and plan of the gardens with the tomb at one end of the four quadrants. The concept of the Paradise Garden is perfected in the gardens of the Taj Mahal. Although based on the classical *charbagh* concept, there is one major difference here, as the monument is placed not at the center but at the end of the garden, forming the perfect climax to the whole design.

Below: The tombs of Shah Jahan and Mumtaz Mahal are enclosed by screens of varying designs in white marble and inlaid with semiprecious stones.

Opposite: The interior chamber of Itmad-ud-Daulah's Tomb in Agra has been finished in white marble with profuse, delicate and intricate stylised inlay and stucco designs. The graves of Nur Jahan's father and mother are made of yellow marble.

Later Mughal Architecture

Moti Masjid in the Red Fort, Delhi.

Bibi ka Maqbara, Aurangabad. Though smaller than the Taj, its disproportionate four minarets make it a poor imitation of its original model.

Aurangzeb

In 1657, Shah Jahan's son Aurangzeb imprisoned him, defeated and killed his elder brother Dara Shikoh and ascended to Delhi's throne. Known equally for piety to the point of intolerance of all other religions, austerity to the point of living like a virtual beggar amidst the splendor of his court, and an unbounded energy to the point of cruelty, Aurangzeb, the last of the Great Mughals, is responsible for the decline of the Mughal empire through his ruinous policies of intolerance.

Aurangzeb was averse to most forms of art, but this aversion did not extend to architecture. However, he frowned upon the use of marble and other luxury materials like sandstone and marble, and favored the use of rough stone and brick. The *pietra dura* work used by his father and grandfather was replaced by decoration in painted stucco. As a result, the fluid lines of Shah Jahan's architecture deteriorated and Aurangzeb's architecture began to become rather heavy. Political events had made a long sojourn into the Deccan necessary and Aurangzeb was influenced by the heavy proportions of the prevailing provincial style. In an effort to counter the loss of architectural grace, there was a concerted move toward excessive ornamentation. Domes became more bulbous, their apex more pronounced, their surfaces fluted and decorated with vertical, horizontal and herringbone stripes, while columns, arches and other elements began to sport incredibly intertwined floral motifs.

The Moti Masjid at Delhi

The Moti Masjid, or Pearl Mosque, was constructed by Aurangzeb within the Red Fort to serve as his private chapel. Situated near his bed chamber, it is a small structure made of white marble, being constructed early in the emperor's reign, before he developed an aversion to the material. It is characterised by a predominance of sinuous contours, and by bulbous domes whose lotus finials are greatly exaggerated.

All the surfaces have curvilinear decoration, including the façades and walls of the courtyard, which are decorated with small arches and columns carved into the marble.

Bibi ka Maqbara

Aurangzeb's wife's tomb, Bibi ka Maqbara, reflects the decay that had set in. It is modeled on the Taj Mahal, but is on a smaller scale. The exaggerated vertical proportions of the tomb, as well as the over-articulation of its form and decorative elements, however, have resulted in the building being without elegance, though not without charm. The tomb is set in a beautifully laid *charbagh*. Compared to the Taj, the mausoleum is rather florid, and without the classic grace that is the hallmark of the earlier examples of the Mughal style.

Architecture after the Mughals

Aurangzeb's death in 1707 saw the great Mughal empire rapidly sliding into decadence and poverty. The century following was probably the most terrible time in India's history, marked by a series of useless battles, excessive debauchery within the court and an impoverished empire. In 1739, Nadir Shah of Persia attacked Delhi and ransacked it, carrying away many treasures, including Shah Jahan's famous Peacock Throne. Delhi also saw the massacre of thousands of her citizens, mercilessly killed by Nadir Shah's mercenaries. It was little wonder

then, that the only significant architectural activity was restricted to the governors of provinces and the Hindu rulers, especially the Rajputs, who had regained their kingdoms from the Mughals.

The Great Imambara at Lucknow

The Bara or Great Imambara at Lucknow is one of the most important examples of the late Mughul style. It was used for the Muharram ceremony, observed by the Shia community to commemorate the martyrdom of Prophet Muhammad's grandson.

Built by Asaf-ud-Daula, one of the Nawabs of Oudh, in 1784 to give employment to workers during a severe famine in the region, the monument is set on one end of a complex with the Asafi Mosque on the opposite end. The complex has two entrances, one functional, the other for the sake of maintaining symmetry. The building is a vaulted hall, 50 meters by 16 meters, rising to over 15 meters. The mosque is placed on a wide, stepped platform. Though rather excessively decorated, it has pleasing proportions. A large hall (50 meters long and 15 meters high) stands unsupported by pillars.

Top left: The Bara or Great Imambara at Lucknow. It is known for its unusual labyrinth of passageways and balconies (*bhoolbhulaiya*) on the upper floor.

Above: The Chhota or Small Imambara at Lucknow. More elegant than its larger counterpart, it is adorned with superb calligraphy and complemented by a lavishly decorated interior.

Provincial Styles

The Provincial styles have been broadly divided into seven categories, depending on the geographic regions of their origin. Broadly based on Indo-Islamic principles that had developed earlier, these styles reflect the cultural and historic influences of their region. Local patronage, climate, availability of material and existing techniques of construction were all contributory factors.

The Malwa Style
(15th to mid-16th century)
The Malwa style, which includes the architecture at Dhar and Mandu in the southern part of central India, is also an offshoot of Sultanate architecture. However, two distinct innovations were developed during its evolution. The combination of the arch, post and lintel was first carried

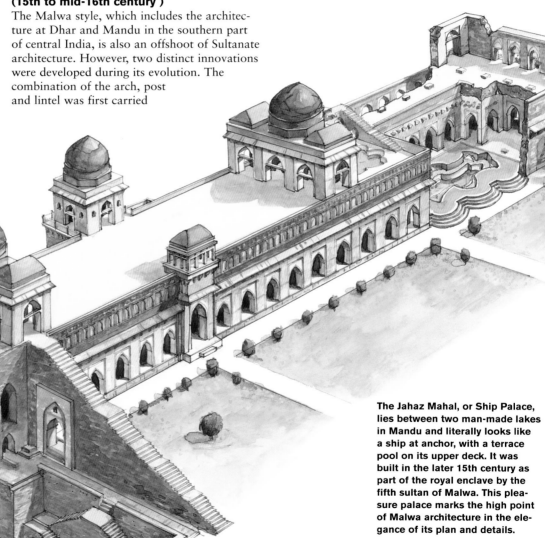

Atala Masjid, Jaunpur. Its most extraordinary feature is the pylon-like *liwan* frontispiece masking the principal and subsidiary *qubbas* of the prayer hall.

The Jahaz Mahal, or Ship Palace, lies between two man-made lakes in Mandu and literally looks like a ship at anchor, with a terrace pool on its upper deck. It was built in the later 15th century as part of the royal enclave by the fifth sultan of Malwa. This pleasure palace marks the high point of Malwa architecture in the elegance of its plan and details.

out here. Mosques were built on a high plinth, ascended by a majestic flight of steps. Colorful semiprecious stones as well as glazed tiles were used in architectural decoration. The Jami Masjid at Mandu is a grand example of this style. Raised on a high plinth, this austere and simple structure has a massive dome over the middle of the *liwan*, while the arcaded gallery around the courtyard is roofed by cylindrical cupolas, except at the corners, where large domes offer a stately profile.

The Punjab Style
(mid-11th to late 16th century)

The region of Punjab, including Multan and Lahore, both now in Pakistan, reflects strong Persian influences. The main building materials used were brick and wood. A distinguishing feature of this style was the doorways, which were intricately carved in distinctive designs, ending in tasselled and knotted patterns, inspired by cloth hangings.

The Jaunpur Style
(late 14th to late 15th century)

Jaunpur was established by Feroze Shah Tughlaq further east near Varanasi but its architecture displays an energy and imagination considerably stronger than the Tughlaq style of Sultanate architecture elsewhere. During its heyday, it was ruled by Muslim rulers of the Sharqi dynasty. The Jaunpur style combined the use of beam and bracket with the arch, and incorporated certain indigenous stylistic mannerisms to create its own distinctive features. The most notable building of this style is the Atala Masjid, erected at the site of an earlier Hindu temple of the same name. Its striking feature is the immense entrance façade that later became the prototype for all religious buildings of the area. Its lower section employs Hindu bracketed openings while higher up, recessed arches, *jharokhas* and *jaalis* fill in the space. On either side of the main entrance are two smaller identical gateways. Each of the remaining three sides of the central courtyard has a similar, though less impressive gateway.

Two other extant mosques in Jaunpur add to its medieval architecture. The first to be built was the Lal Darwaza Masjid, and the last of the three was the Jami Masjid, grander in scale than the Atala Masjid but not nearly as impressive.

The Sharqis were defeated by Bulhul Lodi who, in order to teach them a lesson for attempting to conquer Delhi where the Lodis ruled, razed most of the secular buildings of Jaunpur, except for its mosques, which remain as testimony to the Sharqi's architectural skills.

The Bengal Style
(14th to mid-16th century)

The wet climate was the most important determinant of Bengal's architecture, which is seen mainly in the districts of Gaur and Pandua, capital cities of the Sultanate. It necessitated mosques being built as enclosed spaces, without the customary courtyard, and with narrow entrances that did not allow the rain to enter. Far removed from both Persian and Sultanate influences here, both mosques and tombs incorporated elements from the Hindu temple of Bengal. Lofty walls with arched openings constructed with brick or basalt stone, supported the typical curved *bangla* roof—modeled on the form the bamboo takes when used as roofing. The arches were emphasised with fancy brickwork. The size of domes and vaults was vast. The walls were covered with terracotta panels worked in intricate relief with exotic floral motifs of the region.

Eklakhi Mausoleum, Pandua. Built in the 15th century, it was one of the earliest square brick tombs in Bengal. Pandua replaced Gaur as the capital of Bengal's Muslim rulers. The entrance archway of the inner octagonal chamber surprisingly has a carved image of the Hindu god Ganesh.

Dakhil Darwaza, Gaur. Built in brick in the Bengal tradition by Barbak Shah, the Dakhil Darwaza comprises a central vaulted passage with a series of guard rooms on either side. The entrance façade is rather evocative of the Tughlaq style.

The Gujarat Style
(15th to 16th century)

The most important of the Provincial styles was that of Gujarat. Local architectural traditions were highly developed here and under the Hindu Solanki kings had been well articulated. Above all, Gujarati craftsmen had a refined sense of ancient structural methods and spatial quality.

The city of Ahmedabad was founded by Ahmed Shah in AD 1401 on the left bank of the River Sabarmati. The Muslim Ahmed Shahi rulers had a highly developed aesthetic sensibility and a tremendous interest in architecture. They allowed their zeal to combine with the artistic genius of the Gujarati mason to create buildings that were adaptations and even replicas of Hindu and Jain temples. Although the architectonics of the Islamic *minar*, a vertical element, was not quite understood by the Hindu craftsman of Gujarat, the Islamic element, however, was strongly articulated by the presence of the arch, which alternated with

Top: The Rauza of Ibrahim, Bijapur. The tomb and the mosque stand at either end of an 11-meter-long and 46-meter-wide platform, now surrounded by grass. The ensemble was based on the Mughal "tomb in garden" concept seen at the Taj Mahal.

Above: The screened arcade of the Sidi Sayyid Mosque.

Right: Jami Masjid, Ahmedabad. The arcaded façade screens only the three central zones but there is a clear progression in height from the trabeated outer bays to the arcaded intermediate ones and on to the central frontispiece.

trabeate construction methods. Fine latticework screens or *jaalis* were sensuously carved to fill these spaces, as seen in the Sidi Sayyid Mosque in Ahmedabad, built in the mid-15th century.

The *rauzas* of Gujarat are another unique architectural contribution to the region. The *rauza* comprises a tomb and a mosque facing each other, a strategy employed by the ruling family of Gujarat to create a unified whole and to ensure that the ruler would always be remembered by his people.

The Deccan Style
(mid-14th to late 17th century)

The Persian and Turkish origins of the Deccan rulers is apparent in the style of this region toward the south of India. The first independent dynasty ruled from Gulbarga, shifting to Bidar and finally to Golconda. Deccan architecture incorporated very few indigenous elements. It is characterised by solid buildings of massive proportions that rely on their size to awe the viewer. The often bulbous domes are raised

on high drums, displaying a certain amount of crenellated embellishment to relieve the austerity of the façade. A typical feature of many buildings is the articulation of the base of the drum, in the form of the unfurling lotus.

A formidable repertoire of forts, mosques, mausoleums and *minars* built under successive sovereigns is found in the Deccan region.

The Kashmir Style
(mid-14th to 16th century)

Islamic building traditions in Kashmir were formed as a result of a combination of three different influences: the vernacular building traditions of constructing with wood; the existing traditions of Buddhist and Hindu stone architecture; and the strong influence of Persia and Turkestan where brick, decorated with majolica was used. Architectural elements of mosques and tombs typically included the prayer hall or burial chamber covered by a pyramidal roof; in between the two there was often an open-sided pavilion representing the *minar*.

Top: The Mecca Masjid, Hyderabad. An example of the Deccan style, the Mecca Masjid is one of many mosques built by the former rulers or Nizams of Hyderabad, many of whom are buried here. Extremely affluent, they imported bricks from Mecca, which are embedded in its central arch.

Above: Golconda Fort, the citadel of the Qutab Shahi dynasty who ruled Hyderabad from 1507 to 1687. Built on the site of a 12th-century mud fort, the new monument is a splendid complex of mosques, palaces and gardens.

Left: Jami Masjid, Srinagar, is a complex conforming in general to the court type with cloisters, but the entrances and main prayer halls are *ziarat* pavilions, evocative of village shrines.

Sacred Sikh Architecture

The building of the Golden Temple in Amritsar (elevation below) was started in the late 16th century. It was rebuilt in 1764 and the marble and gold embellishments (opposite far right) were added in the early 19th century. Most other *gurudwaras* in India are modeled on the Golden Temple.

Opposite left: The central hall of the Golden Temple, with the *Granth Sahib* under a golden canopy. Delicate inlay work of ivory and mirror and elegantly molded stucco come together to create an extravagant and opulent interior.

Founded toward the end of the 15th century by Guru Nanak, Sikhism was a reformist, monotheistic religion, a reaction to the inequalities that prevailed under the caste system of Hinduism. Later, it acquired a militant character in opposition to the religious zealotry of Aurangzeb under whom the Mughal empire began its decline, and when provincial rulers, such as the Sikhs in Punjab, established themselves.

After Nanak, Sikhism was further expounded by nine *gurus* or teachers, the third of whom established the sacred city of Amritsar, and the fourth compiled the hymns of the *gurus* in the *Adi Granth*; to house these, he built the Golden Temple at Amritsar. The last of the *gurus*, Guru Gobind Singh, founded the brotherhood of the Khalsa in 1699 as a military order to fight oppression, and gave the religion its present guidelines, which include the concept of the *sanghat*, or congregation, sharing of all resources and living by honest, hard work. He also reorganised the *Adi Granth*, renaming it the *Guru Granth Sahib*, which occupies the most inviolable place in a Sikh *gurudwara*.

The Gurudwara

The *gurudwara*, which literally means "the threshold (*dwara*) of the *guru*," is the Sikh temple, an architectural embodiment of the tenets of Sikhism. All visitors, irrespective of caste or creed, are given shelter here and provided with food. Visitors are required to remove their shoes, wash their feet and cover their heads before entering the precincts.

The concept of a community in which all are equal is emphasised by the total absence of special enclosures in the *gurudwara*. A tank is always provided at the entrance for ritual washing of the feet. The central space consists of a large hall, which houses the *Granth Sahib* and where congregational prayer takes place. An essential part of the *gurudwara*, often a separate building, is the *langar*, or kitchen, which provides free food to worshippers.

The Golden Temple of Amritsar is the main shrine of the Sikhs. It was built at ground level rather than on a high plinth in keeping with the Sikh spirit of humility. A 20-square-meter platform in the middle of a large *sarovar* or tank is the base on which it stands. A causeway measuring 62 meters in length and 6.5 meters in width links the main entrance to the temple across the tank. The three-storied structure is decorated with cusped arches, ribbed domes, *chhattris* and *jaalis*. The marble-clad façade is covered with delicate relief work and the domes with gold leaf.

The architecture of the *gurudwara* displays Mughal and Rajput influences: arches, a profusion of *chhattris*, a lotus-finialed ribbed dome, the use of marble and decorative motifs in *pietra dura*, and small balconied windows protected by shallow *chhajjas* or parapets.

Maharaja Ranjit Singh consolidated Sikh power in the Punjab in the early 19th century and is responsible for the finest examples of Sikh sacred and other architecture built in the region. The Golden Temple, which was sacked and rebuilt in 1764, was given its final embellishments in gold and marble by Ranjit Singh.

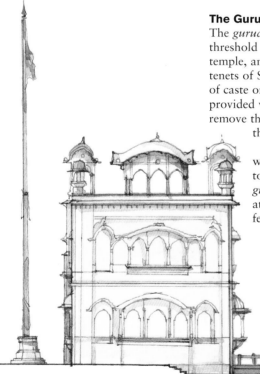

Secular Spaces: The Fort

Even while sacred architecture formed a large part of India's varied architectural language, secular architecture further enriched its aesthetic vocabulary. Spaces created for royalty, especially forts, citadels and palaces, reflect the security needs and lifestyles of rulers who, regardless of which religion they belonged to, had common aspirations for power and the desire to leave their footprint on history.

The concept of the fort or citadel is codified in the *Artha Shastra*, an ancient treatise on the laws and strategies of statecraft, written by the Mauryan chancellor Chanakya, also known as Kautilya. Chanakya studied the systems of defense required in different situations and classified fortified establishments on the basis of the geography of suitable sites, as well as on elements and strategies of defense.

Rajasthan, a region where the Aravalli hills extend outward into the scrubland in rocky, formidable outcrops, and also where strong clan loyalties exist, abounds in forts. Initially barren and forbidding, as most Rajput forts are, they gradually acquired a more habitable image as the Rajputs and their prime adversaries, the Mughals, made peace with each other. Opulent living quarters, pavilions and gardens were added and the architecture even adopted elements from Islamic buildings.

Classification of Forts
Forts or *durgs* were divided into six main types: the *dhanva durg* or desert fort, which relied on its hostile location for defense (e.g. Jaisalmer, see pp. 108–9); the *giri durg* or hill fort, which was situated on a high, relatively impregnable rocky outcrop, thus eliminating the element of surprise (e.g. Kumbhalgarh); the *jala durg* or water fort, situated amidst a river or deep lake or on the sea (e.g. the forts of the Marathas built in the western coastal areas); the *vana durg* or forest fort, which used the camouflage as well as the hostility of unknown forests for protection (e.g. Ranthambhore, Rajasthan); the *mahi durg* or mud fort, which used extraordinarily massive mud walls that were capable of withstanding the onslaught of cannons (e.g. Bharatpur's Lohagarh); the *nara durg*, a city fort which made use of a large army to protect it in situations without any particular advantage of location (e.g. Agra Fort).

In addition, Chanakya spelt out elaborate arrangements for defense. For example, for the *nara durg*, he specified that the ramparts should be surrounded by three ditches, spiked and variously filled with sand, mud and flowing water, as well as with crocodiles. The ramparts should be planted with poisonous bushes and crowned by several ringed walls of brick, graded in height and twice as high as they are broad.

Features of the Fort
Ramparts and outer fortified walls had walkways wide enough to accommodate patrols in both directions. These were interrupted by watchtowers at regular intervals. The ramparts also had a complex system of tunnels and staircases to allow carriers of messages and reinforcements to other parts of the fort. The design of the ramparts and battlements was further refined according to the weapons deployed. In the days of bows and arrows, these contained narrow slits that allowed only the arrow to project out. This became a stylistic motif as well. Later, with the introduction of gunpowder and cannons into India by Emperor Babur, the ramparts were designed to accommodate both cannon and men, without interfering with the requirements of width for patrolling. Walls were made accordingly, and later forts have massive walls to withstand cannon fire.

Forts were entered through massive fortified gates, flanked by watchtowers linked by passages and large enough for elephants to pass (as in Bundi, Rajasthan). Most forts had a series of gates, which were often commemorative of victories in battle. The shutters were made of huge planks of wood, reinforced by spikes and metal bands. Within the shutters was a smaller door, usually with a high sill and low lintel, through which a single man could pass. The paths that led to the gates were often steep and winding to slow down the progress of attackers.

Top: The Vijay Stambh or Victory Tower in the fort of Chittorgarh, Rajasthan, was built by Maharana Kumbha between 1458 and 1468 to commemorate his victory over Sultan Mahmud of Malwa.

Above: The massive fortified entrance gate to the Bundi Fort in Rajasthan

All forts had a special area for worship. In Hindu forts, this was usually a temple dedicated to the principal deity of the ruling clan.

The armory or Sileh Khana, which housed all the arms and ammunition, was always located in a strategic place, and its keeper was a trusted member of the ruling family. The granary had to be large enough to house immense amounts of food grains, that were required for the occupants of the fort to withstand long days of siege. The Naqqar or Naubat Khana was a gallery where massive ceremonial drums were kept and were used to signal danger, victory and social events.

The Living Quarters

The location of the palace or living quarters of the royal occupants of the fort was in its most protected area. The palace consisted of men's quarters, known as the *mardana*, and separate women's quarters, known as the *zenana*, which usually occupied the innermost section. The chambers comprised passages linking the various rooms, to facilitate escape, and areas where the king would grant audiences.

A complex arrangement of rooms, twisting passages and narrow hidden staircases was the hallmark of Rajput palaces built during times of danger. The Rajputs, known for their valor, did not flee from the enemy, and if they lost a battle, their women and children, rather than facing capture, immolated themselves in a ritual collective burning known as *jauhar*. At Chittorgarh in Rajasthan, one such *jauhar* saw nearly 30,000 women and children fling themselves into blazing fires lit in underground chambers which were specially designed for this purpose.

Above: The ruined ramparts and outer walls of a hill fort.

Below: Kumbhalgarh, a magnificent mountain fort in the Mewar region of Rajasthan, sprawls across the hills on a plateau over 1000 meters high. Built by Rana Kumbha in 1458, the invincibility of the fort is underscored by the fact that it was sacked just once in its history, by the combined might of the Mughals and the rulers of Amber and Marwar, who poisoned its water source.

Secular Spaces: The Palace

Earlier palaces were located within fortified citadels. Built during times of strife, their planning and construction reflected the need for protection from enemies. However, the shifting of alliances and political events soon resulted in a decreasing need for such heavily fortified palaces. Where war had dictated the architecture of the palace earlier, it was peace times that allowed its subsequent evolution.

Certain spatial components, nevertheless, remained common to palaces in times of both war and peace, and these, along with an inherent sensitivity to design, excellent craftsmanship and ornate decoration, defined the living spaces of royalty throughout India.

The Public Area
The audience hall was the main component of the public area within the palace, where the king would hold his court, known as the durbar, receive visitors and messengers, and conduct the business of the day. The Mughals further redefined the concept of the audience hall, and created the Diwan-i-Am, or the Hall of Public Audience, and the Diwan-i-Khas, or the Hall of Private Audience, to which entry was privileged. The audience hall was sumptuously decorated, and its focal point was invariably the throne. During British rule, the audience halls of palaces came to be known as Durbar Halls and were used to receive representatives of the Raj.

The Royal Chambers
The royal chambers of the king and members of the royal family constituted a large spatial component of the palace and exhibited, along with a lavishness in decoration, the idiosyncrasies of individual rulers. Often added to by successive kings, the living area was divided into the *mardana* or men's quarters, and the *zenana* or women's quarters, in keeping with the social practice of *purdah*—segregation on the basis of gender, which was practiced by Hindus and Muslims alike. The residents of the *zenana* included not only the official queens but also the king's extensive harem. The windows of the *zenana* were covered with stone latticework screens to ensure privacy for the womenfolk.

Each queen as well as the king's favorite concubines, had residential complexes assigned to them, guarded by trusted eunuchs. The royal children were born and grew up here, and male heirs were given rooms in the *mardana* only after they had reached a certain age.

The City Palace in Udaipur, Rajasthan, one of the largest palace complexes in the country. It is, in fact, a series of several palaces, such as the Bada Mahal, Dilkush Mahal, Krishna Mahal, Manek Mahal and the Chini Chitrashala (decorated in Chinese and Dutch tiles), added on by successive maharajas.

Other Areas

A special feature of many palaces was the Sheesh Mahal, or Palace of Mirrors, an exclusive chamber where surfaces were inlaid with glass and mirror, colored and plain, convex and flat, so that the light from one candle was reflected in a thousand different patterns.

The rooms of a palace were usually arranged around enclosed and secluded courtyards, all knitted together in a freely arranged system, often at various levels. The *zenana* had roofed terraces and enclosed gardens, extravagantly laid out, with water fountains and pleasure pavilions. The living area often included a private shrine or space for prayer.

The treasury and service areas, such as the stables, kitchens, granary and housing for servants, were included in the outer court and formed the rest of the palace complex.

Love for the ornate, often bordering on a pretentiousness, was reflected in lavish decorations and embellishments, with walls, ceilings and floors providing the canvas for painted murals, carving, and gilt and inlay work.

Elevation and plan of the Govind Mahal in Datia, Madhya Pradesh. The palace was built by a Bundela king in 1620. The dense five-storied structure has richly painted royal apartments, and a central courtyard connected by double-storied bridges to the galleries around. There is also an extensive network of underground chambers.

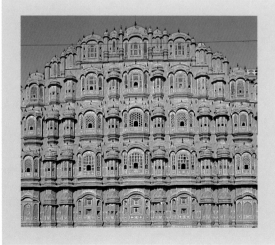

The Hawa Mahal

Hawa Mahal, literally "the Palace of the Wind," was an architectural response to the needs of Rajput Hindu women of the royal family, who were required to stay within the confines of the palace but wished to participate in what was happening in the world outside. The element of the screened opening, open to the wind, ensured that women were not seen while they observed public events. In 1799, Raja Pratap Singh, the Maharaja of Jaipur, commissioned the construction of a building that was specially designed for women of the royal household to watch life in the street and colorful state processions as they passed by. Jaipur's Hawa Mahal, at the crossroads of two of the city's most important thoroughfares, is five stories high, but only one room wide. Its ornate façade is a series of small windows, each opening emphasised by *bangla* roofs and small canopies or *chhattris*, and covered with trellised screens. The building, with slim walls only 20 centimeters thick, is constructed of lime mortar and painted pink on the outside to simulate the red sandstone of the city's architecture. The ornate façade is embellished with delicate white-painted tracery.

The Rajput Fort and Palace

Above and below: The towering citadel of Mehrangarh sits high on a 125-meter-high hill. Its powerful walls run 10 kilometers all around and reach a height of up to 45 meters. The ramparts are wide with cannons placed at strategic intervals.

Mehrangarh

Mehrangarh Fort, built by the Rajput king Rao Jodha in 1458, and added to by successive generations, is situated on a formidable outcrop of rock and commands an uninterrupted view of the entire countryside, denying any attacker the element of surprise.

Its steep approach twists and turns in a series of sharp bends, through a succession of seven gates, until the last gate, the Suraj Pol (Sun Gate), allows entry into the main area of the fort, famous both for its fortifications and for its exquisite palaces. The fort is built of deep red and pale-colored sandstone and is distinguished by a series of stark, formidable bastions over which hang delicately wrought and intricately carved balconies. The main court of the palace complex, known as the Shringar Chowk, contains the white marble throne of the dynasty, which is still used when conducting the ceremony to anoint the head of the clan. The Shringar Chowk is surrounded by large reception rooms which constitute the public area of the fort. The complex contains a series of palaces and courtyards at various levels, with an intricate system of staircases which would succeed in disorienting any outsider.

The façades of the complex, with projecting windows supported on carved corbels, roofed over with stone replicas of the *bangla* roof, portray an elaborately embellished expanse which gives no clue to the arrangement of rooms behind. Among the palaces is the Sheesh Mahal, or Glass Palace, which has a ceiling covered with glass balls as well as glass mosaic on the walls. The Phool Mahal, or Flower Palace, has stucco walls and ceilings that are covered with exquisite paintings framed by floral borders. The Jhanki Mahal, or Tableau Palace, has mirrors embedded into the walls opposite the windows, enabling the women to see what was happening in the court below without being seen themselves. The Zenana Mahal is another palace with its own enclosed garden. The temple dedicated to the family deity is also located here.

Jaisalmer

The foundations of the desert fort of Jaisalmer, located on the trade route between the Gangetic plain and Sind to the west, were laid in AD 1198 by Raja Jaisal of the Rajput Bhatti clan. Built amongst the sand dunes of the Thar desert, the fort remained intact for nearly 800 years both due to its impregnable architecture and because the Bhatti kings were not involved in the battles for supremacy common in Rajasthan's history.

The fort is built entirely of yellow sandstone blocks, without the use of any mortar, held together by iron clamps which did not rust in the dry desert air. The 99 bastions of the outer wall are built in a sinuous curve and the main entrance of the fort is a massive fortified gate. Within the fort walls are the palace of the *maharawal* (as the ruler was known in this region). It contains several chambers, a drum gallery, a coronation square atop a wide flight of open stairs, numerous Jain temples, and a granary. However, it is the *havelis* (mansions) of the merchants, who were promoted to the status of hereditary prime minister, that constitute Jaisalmer's most celebrated buildings—splendidly stone carved alongside narrow streets.

Left and below: The Jaisalmer citadel is surrounded by an inner defensive wall which dominates the settlement on the northern side. The settlement had its own protective wall, much of which is now in ruins. This is one of the few ancient Indian forts that is still inhabited, by almost 8,000 people, who live in houses tightly packed together within the walls of the fort. Cenotaphs (below left) dot the scrubland around.

Below right: Plan of the triangular hill which forms the upper section and focus of Jaisalmer, showing the arrangement of streets and squares.

Painted and decorated interior
of the Phool Mahal (Flower
Palace) in the Mehrangarh Fort
at Rajasthan, one of a series of
palaces within the fort complex.
The stucco walls and ceilings are
covered with exquisite paintings
framed by floral borders.

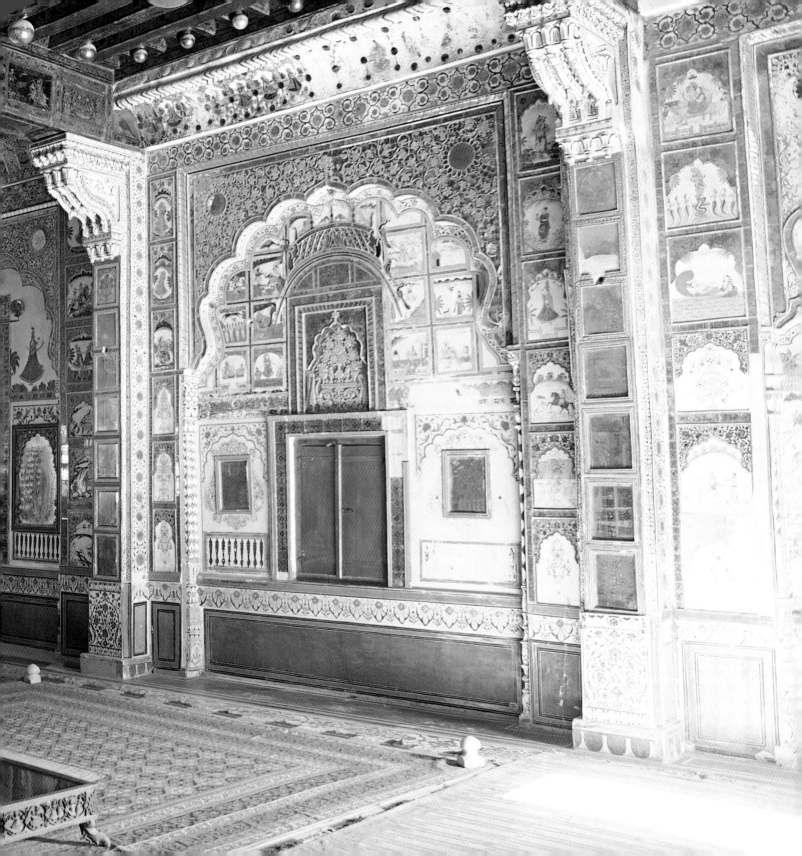

The Gwalior Fort and Palace

Eastward from Rajasthan, across the Chambal River, lies the city of Gwalior, gateway to central India. Its most outstanding monument is the massive Gwalior Fort, stretching 3 kilometers across a 100-meter-high rocky plateau.

The Fort

The foundations for Gwalior's hill fort were probably laid by a Rajput prince in the 9th century. Owing to its strategic location, it passed through the hands of many rulers of various Rajput clans, and in between, the Sultanate dynasty, until it finally became the base for the Scindias, the most powerful of a confederate of Hindu dynasties from the Deccan region. The building is thus an interesting amalgam of Hindu, Jain and Islamic architecture.

Access to the fort, surrounded by fortifications that run around the entire plateau, is through a typically tortuous route interspersed by several gates. Along one route are caves once inhabited by Jain ascetics and lined with 15th-century sculptures of the Jain *tirthankaras*. The more common route, which passes by five gates, culminates in the final portal, the Hathia Pol or Elephant Gate, which is contiguous with the stone façade of the spectacular Man Mandir palace behind.

Man Mandir (Palace)

Man Mandir was built by the Tomar king Raja Man Singh in the 15th century. Entrance to it is flanked by twin turrets; both the portal and the façade of the palace retain much of the original blue, white and yellow tilework. A covered, corridor-like room connects the two turrets.

The palace has two main courtyards, around which the various sections are built to a height

Above and right: The ancient hill fort of Gwalior (layout below), lying directly on the main route from the north to the south, is the gateway to central India. Its late 15th-century Man Mandir palace is the oldest Hindu secular building in India which still remains virtually intact. Its façades retain the original rich blue, white and yellow tilework.

of two floors. Audience halls and chambers constitute the main level. The upper floor, which housed the *zenana*, has a series of surrounding passages, as well as roof terraces and pavilions that overlook the courts through screened galleries. The floor of the main level projects out to create deep eaves which are supported on carved brackets. The massive exterior of the palace does not reflect the essentially human scale of the apartments within, which are richly varied in both volume and ornament. Deep subterranean chambers, used as retreats in summer, lie toward one end, beneath the main level. Below this, on the second level, are the dungeons.

Other Buildings

The Gwalior Fort encompasses six palaces, three temples and several water tanks. Teli ka Mandir, on the south side, is the oldest surviving building

in the fort and the tallest. The 9th-century shrine, dedicated to Shakti, the divine female energy, has an unusual double oblong *shikhara*. It is capped with a vaulted arch roof, rising to about 25 meters, which recalls the *chaitya* windows of earlier Buddhist rock-cut caves. The central area of the temple projects forward, stepped in elevation under superimposed horseshoe-window motifs. The superstructure covers a closed portico.

The Sas Bahu (mother- and daughter-in-law) Temples are two elegant temples of the 11th century, somewhat reminiscent of the Khajuraho style (see pp. 64–5), the larger going up to three floors in the central section. At the foot of the plateau is Gujari Mahal, which was built for a particular queen of Raja Man Singh who was not allowed to reside in the palaces within the fort because she belonged to a lower caste.

Top: The smaller of the Sas Bahu temples within Gwalior Fort. The *mandapa* is an open pavilion here, much like those seen in Khajuraho. Its pyramidal roof is covered by bell-shaped sections. Sculpted pillars in the interior are seen to good effect as it is half open all around, creating a feeling of lightness.

Above left and right: Carved columns and ceilings decorate the interior of the Man Mandir palace. Inner spaces are flat-roofed, except for one chamber, which has a false ribbed vault. Structurally, the palace combines the native trabeate and imported arcuate systems.

Palaces of South India

Top and above: Roof motif and detail, Padmanabhapuram Palace.

Below: Section of the Mother Palace, which had intricate woodwork and red floors perfectly polished with hibiscus flowers.

The Padmanabhapuram Palace

Padmanabhapuram, in the state of Tamil Nadu, was the capital of Travancore (now in Kerala) between 1550 to 1570. The palace was the residence of the maharaja and epitomises Kerala architecture in its form, building craft and use of materials. It underwent extensive rebuilding and restoration in the 18th century, carried out by the ruler, Marthanda Varma.

The palace complex consists of a number of individual buildings, and a profile of the exterior depicts gently pitched tiled roofs broken by triangular gables projecting over delicately carved screens. The complex includes all the statutory elements of a palace, public ceremonial spaces, a mint, an armory, a picture and manuscript gallery, a dance hall and temples, all of which, at varying heights, from one to several floors, are set around a series of courtyards.

The principal variant here is the importance in size and focus given to the queen mother's, or matriarch's quarters, which derives from the state's matrilineal system. The king's apartments, called the *rajanivesana*, may occupy a higher elevation, on the fourth floor, but they are relatively isolated, and connected only by a long corridor skirting the women's more easily accessible quarters on the ground floor, with the hall of private audience. Walls made of teak rest on granite plinths. In many areas the walls are not solid but are constructed in a system of open struts and slats, which, like the gables, allow the enclosed spaces to be well ventilated. The interiors are gently lit through windows made of teak frames and mullions within which thin, translucent bits of shell were inserted, instead of glass. The black floor is polished with a painstaking technique, now lost, using a special mixture of coconut oil, charcoal, lime, palm toddy, egg white and certain plant resins.

Painted murals and fine examples of wooden carving adorn the interiors of all the buildings. Each intersection of rafters and purlins displays a variation of the lotus motif.

The Royal Center at Hampi

The Royal Center at Hampi, originally the seat of the southern Vijayanagara empire (see p. 54), saw an integration of different architectural styles with successive rulers. As it stands today, it contains buildings that are Hindu as well as Islamic in style. It is surrounded by long rambling walls that follow the contours of the outcrops of rocks and boulders. These walls are

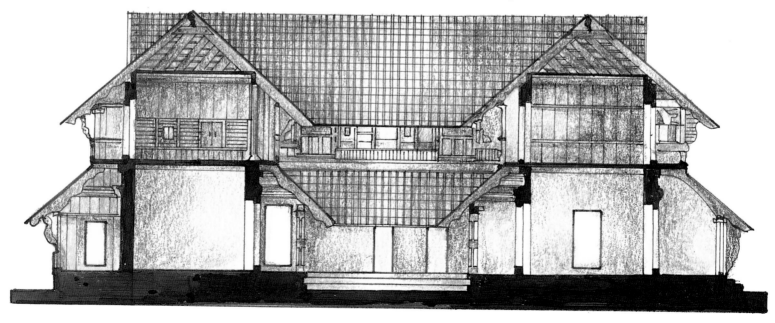

pierced by several gates, which vary from simple trabeate structures to more elaborate edifices with corbels, arches and even domes.

The original complex consisted of three distinct areas, the ceremonial court, the palace compounds and the *zenana*, which were laid out in perpendicular axes aligned to cardinal points. At the intersection of each was a temple.

Within the ceremonial court are two monumental platforms. The larger of the two forms the plinth of the king's audience hall, which was a great hypostyle hall whose roof rested on ten rows of timber columns. The hall has since been destroyed.

The second tiered platform is known as the Mahanavami Dibba or the Throne Platform. This 12-meter-high pyramidal structure was the place from where the king, seated on a high throne, viewed the ceremonies and processions of the dynastic cult festival of Mahanavami. The sides of the platform are sculpted with friezes show-ing scenes associated with this festival.

To the west of the ceremonial court are two compounds that contain the king's private apartments and those of the *zenana*. All the buildings rest on stepped and terraced platforms. The inner chambers were multistoried structures in stone and timber, partitioned by plastered brick walls and preceded by either a court or a hall.

One of the few buildings that remains intact within the complex is the Lotus Mahal. This has a series of cruciform projections in plan. Designed like a *mandapa*, with conical *shikharas* over arcaded openings, it probably functioned like a *hawa mahal* (see p. 107). The form of the Lotus Mahal is a striking blend of the Hindu and Islamic styles.

Other buildings that survive are the elephants' stables, the guard house and the queen's bath. The elephants' stables are a row of massive rooms, with domes in alternating variations of form. The queen's bath is a huge tank, whose inner sides form an intricate pattern of steps.

Elephant Stables, Hampi. The elevation displays distinctly Islamic features, such as curved openings, recessed lobed arches and domes. An overhanging eave and parapet surmounts the walls. The tower rising above the upper chamber has now collapsed.

Lotus Mahal, Hampi. A two-storied pleasure palace, it is a harmonious synthesis of both Hindu and Muslim architectural features.

Fatehpur Sikri

In 1568, Emperor Akbar, who was without an heir, prayed at the hermitage of the Sufi saint Shaikh Salim Chisti in the village of Sikri, near Agra. The saint's prophecy of heirs was partly fulfilled a year later with the birth of a son, who was named Salim after the saint, but later called Jahangir. Two years later, Akbar built a city at the saint's abode, and named it Fatehpur.

Top: The 54-meter-high Buland Darwaza was erected by Akbar to commemorate his conquest of Gujarat. It leads into the vast courtyard of the Jami Masjid.

Above: The unusual central pillar in the Diwan-i-Khas with its carved corbels.

Right: Anup Talao, a pool where Akbar's renowned court musician Tansen would perform on the central platform to such perfection that legend says oil lamps would alight with his singing. The building to its north, seen here, is the Diwan-i-Khas, and to the west lies the Panch Mahal, the five-storied open-air pavilion.

The city was constructed in a record time of fifteen years. A huge artificial lake was first created by damming a seasonal river, and a complex system of cisterns and tanks was fed from this. Built within a rectangle measuring about 2 by 3 kilometers, the city was surrounded on three sides by an unfortified wall.

The design and construction of Fatehpur Sikri is a true reflection of Akbar's eclectic spirit. Architects and artists from all over India were invited to participate, and while the guidelines were clearly laid down by Akbar, individual buildings appear to have come up spontaneously as pragmatic responses to functional needs. Orientation, topography, issues of security and aesthetics all governed the architecture. All important structures lie along the cardinal axes. A north–south axis defines buildings of a secular nature while the Jami Masjid is symmetrically built on an east–west axis as required by Islam.

The central part of the city was divided into three complexes. The Sacred Complex, containing the Great Mosque or Jami Masjid, entered through a massive victory gateway, the Buland Darwaza. It also houses the tomb of Salim Chisti (see pp. 88–9), and a smaller mosque called the Sangatarashan or Stonemasons' Mosque.

The Royal Complex consists of the palace of Jodha Bai, Akbar's Rajput queen and Jahangir's mother; the palace of Raja Birbal, who was one of the luminaries of Akbar's court; and the palaces of Akbar's Christian queen Maryam and Turkish queen known as the Turkish Sultana.

The third distinct area of the central part is the Public Court. This contains the Panch Mahal, a building with five successively dimin-

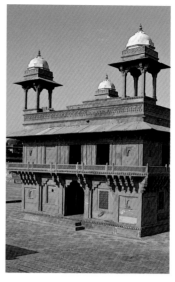

ishing stories, Akbar's private apartments known as the Khwabgah, or House of Dreams, and the halls of public and private audience, or the Diwan-i-Am and Diwan-i-Khas. Within the Diwan-i-Khas is a spectacular freestanding single stone column. Its capital supports a platform linked to the four sides of its containing chamber by open courses at the level of the first floor. It was here that the emperor sat with his ministers, overlooking those below who sought special audience with him.

The city also contained residences for nobles of the court, houses for artists, musicians and intellectuals, and more modest homes for those who served the emperor. Other buildings in the Public Court are baths, cisterns, a girls' school, and the drum gallery or Naubat Khana. Service areas were located on the outskirts.

The entire city, strongly influenced by the building traditions of Gwalior, Rajasthan, Gujarat and Malwa, is built of red sandstone, much favored by Akbar. He brought artisans from every part of his empire to work on it. Fifteen years after it was built, the city was abandoned. The reasons for this are still unclear. Some attribute it to an acute shortage of water, while others contend that political considerations made Akbar shift his capital to Lahore before choosing to return again to Agra, but not to Fatehpur Sikri.

Above left: The Panch Mahal.

Above: The Diwan-I-Khas, or Hall of Private Audience.

Below: A drawing of the palace of Raja Birbal, Akbar's adviser and confidante.

The Salim Chisti mausoleum at Fatehpur Sikri is built entirely of white marble and is a complete contrast to the rest of the buildings in the sprawling complex, which are made of red sandstone. The marble shrine is the spiritual center of Fatehpur Sikri and is one of the best examples of marble work in the world.

Colonial Architecture

Architecture has always been a symbol of power, designed to endorse the might of the patron. By the time the Europeans arrived, several outsiders had invaded India and created architectural styles reflective of their original and adopted homes. The European colonisers created an architecture that was a symbol of their mission of conquest, whether it be dedicated to the Church or to the State.

Church of our Lady of the Angels in Pondicherry, a French settlement established by Francois Martin in 1674.

Early European Powers

The quest for gold, glory and God drove the nations of post-Renaissance Europe to discover new lands. The Portuguese, the Dutch, the British and the French, all came to India with perhaps different intents, but their architectural articulation was based on the same principle of establishing their identity and authority.

The Portuguese, led by Vasco da Gama in 1498, were the first to come to India, and were more driven by a Catholic missionary zeal than a desire for lasting political control. Their first, and indeed, most glorious buildings were churches, cathedrals, basilicas and seminaries.

The British, who, by the beginning of the 17th century had established the East India Company, formally made India a colony of the British Empire in 1857. By this time, their presence had been architecturally established through the construction of a host of buildings, including forts, garrison churches and civic structures. The architecture that they created, both before and after 1857, was an expression of the power of the state, and the term "colonial" or "imperial" is commonly understood to refer to this phase of architecture in India.

British Architecture

Although at the time of Britain's colonising activities in the subcontinent there was a move in England and Europe to incorporate "exotic" oriental elements into the prevalent neoclassical style to create the Ecclesiastic movement, the British in India departed from this norm. One of the salient features of colonial or imperial architecture was that it enthusiastically espoused the moral and aesthetic values of a Christian civilisation, synonymous in British eyes with "civilised" society, and rejected any local element as reflective of a native "barbarism."

The fort of Diu was built on the Gulf of Cambay by the Portuguese. Protected by the sea on three sides, this citadel is fortified by a deep moat on the fourth side, and has sea-facing cannons mounted on its ramparts.

Thus, to begin with, colonial buildings were built in a pure rendering of different classical styles where clear lines, imposing pediments and white surfaces reflected the power and dignity of Greek and Roman originals. In England, the Gothic style was being revived, and the British Perpendicular Gothic, the chosen style for most civic buildings made in the mid-1800s in India, necessitated the use of imported glass. Climatic conditions of India, however, made it imperative for them to adapt the forms and styles of medieval Europe to the functional requirements of the subcontinent. This adaptation marked the beginning of a hybridisation of Indian and European stylistic elements, leading to the creation of what is now referred to as the Indo-Saracenic style. The range of this style is wide indeed, from incorporating a few Indian decorative elements into a basic Gothic building, to a full-blown synthesis of both traditions. The fusion of the two traditions, though awkward and self-conscious at first, found its balance in the architecture of Sir Edwin Lutyens, in his design of the capital city of New Delhi (see p. 136).

Colonial architecture encompassed a wide range of buildings, from churches to warehouses. British architecture, in turn, influenced native rulers to adopt Western palace types in whole or part. Elements such as salons and banqueting halls were freely introduced to cater to the new needs of entertaining Western guests.

Above: Bronze statue of Queen Victoria by Sir George Frampton, Victoria Memorial, Calcutta.

Above left: Imperial Lodge, Simla, was designed by Henry Irwin in the Elizabethan or English Renaissance style with hardly any Indian influence visible in its detailing or form. It now houses the Institute of Advanced Studies.

Painting by James Baillie Fraser (1890) of the Government House, Calcutta, built by Charles Wyatt. Based on Kedleston Hall, Derbyshire, it is well adapted to the vagaries of the Bengal climate, with wide verandahs and a colonnade on the south front.

The Colonial Church

Led by the Portuguese, the Europeans, in the 15th century, established colonies along the coasts of India according to the various concessions granted to them. The Portuguese, whose mercantile zeal was equaled by the Christian zeal of their missionaries, built many splendid cathedrals and churches in Goa.

These were built typically in the European Classicist and Baroque styles, with the plan and elements often culled from pattern books, which were collections of plan elevations and details from seminal buildings all over Europe. The colonial architect often used these books as a source of inspiration. The synthesis of otherwise different elements is therefore seen in many Christian buildings in India.

Even today, the greatest monuments to Christianity that exist in India were those built by the Portuguese in Goa, although the British church, too, occupies a distinct place in the architectural history of the country.

The Basilica of Bom Jesus, Goa

When they arrived in 1498, the Portuguese were the first to introduce Catholicism to India. Francis Xavier, a contemporary and colleague of Ignatius Loyola (founder of the Jesuit order) came to Goa in AD 1542. A life-size image of the bearded monk, made of painted wood, stands in the robing room of the Church of Bom Jesus (Good Jesus) in Goa, and his remains are enshrined in a side chapel of the church, covered with panels relating to his life and miracles.

The church was completed in 1605. It is built of laterite and plaster and has a three-storied Renaissance façade. The main altar depicts the infant Jesus under the protection of St Ignatius Loyola, and in the southern transept with twisted gilded columns is the Chapel and Tomb of St Francis Xavier. The interior is ornamented with wood and gold leaf, characteristic of the "Indian Baroque" style. All three classical orders of columns—Doric, Ionic and

Corinthian—find expression in the church. The Portuguese were clearly bent on emphasising their lofty heritage and superiority over native architectural traditions.

St Andrew's Kirk, Madras

St Andrew's Kirk, in Madras, consecrated in 1821, was based on the design of St Martins-in-the Fields, London. Thomas de Havilland and James Caldwell of the Madras Engineers modified the original design to make it structurally suited to the marshy site on which the church was built. The foundations of St Andrew's Kirk, considered to be the finest British church built in India in the 19th century, are a series of deep wells, some made of brick and others of specially designed pottery cylinders, dug so that the high water table would not damage the building or cause the foundation to sink.

The building itself is basically circular in form, one of only three churches in India which has a circular seating plan. It is axially flanked by two rectangular compartments, one of which contains the deep entrance porch. The porch is surrounded by a double colonnade of twelve massive Ionic columns, and surmounted by a pediment. One of the façades has a pediment flanked by two British lions, and the motto of the East India Company engraved on it.

The main chamber measures 25 meters in diameter. It is roofed by a shallow dome and supported by an annular arch, made of specially designed hollow pottery cones, on which rest sixteen columns with Corinthian capitals. The interior of the dome is painted blue with a special mixture made of crushed seashell and lapis lazuli, and decorated with gold stars.

A staircase leads onto the flat roof and continues past the clock on all four sides, past the massive bell and up the tall spire onto a small balcony from which you can overlook the entire city. The staircase in the spire contains fine wooden balustrades.

The concessions made by the builders to the hot tropical climate can be seen in the cool checkered floor of black and white marble, the cane pews and louvered doors. A magnificent stained-glass window provides a focal point within the church.

The Colonial Fort

Early postcard of the Hooghly River with the High Court in the background.

The early architectural needs of the colonial powers who came to India were manifested in buildings catering to their mercantile needs. Later, as the need to fortify these became necessary, protected garrisons emerged that housed not only warehouses but also residential and official quarters for officers and soldiers, churches, banks and theaters. Thus, Fort St William was built to house the entire European community. It was modeled on state-of-the-art European forts with ramparts, redoubts, ditches and earthworks.

The Portuguese introduced at Daman the star-shaped plan of the ideal fortified city of Vitruvius. British and French forts were based on the 17th-century planning principles perfected by Vauban, a French military engineer. Regular polygonal geometry with triangular bastions at each angle maximised all-round cover and protected the curtain wall. Forts built at Madras, Bombay and Calcutta consisted of double walls and angular bastions built low for the artillery to command the level of approach.

Fort St George, Madras

Built in the mid-17th century, Fort St George at Madras is the oldest fort to be built by the East India Company. Within its stellar fortifications, separated from the native settlement that lay outside, was the European settlement. The area within the fort was known as White Town, and the Indian township outside was called Black Town.

Within the fort there was a clear demarcation of space. The military garrison lay beneath the walls, while the civilians lived near the warehouses. This division was the beginning of a later well-established separation in all British settlements in India, with the military area coming to be known as the Cantonment.

Within 60 years, Fort St George grew into a major city with 300,000 inhabitants and well-planned streets lined with trees on a grid-iron pattern. The town planning of Fort St George, which up to the present remains the seat of government, is the first instance of large-scale English town planning principles in India.

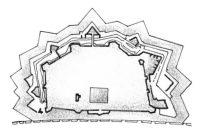

Plan of Fort St George reflects the star shape in part, which allowed for angular bastions and protected recessed flanks. In the 1750s, when the British recovered it from the French, it was redesigned in its present semi-octagonal form by the eminent military mathematician, Benjamin Robins, and even enclosed an exchange, auction rooms and a subscription library.

Fort St George by Jan van Ryne in 1754, showing public buildings, including St Mary's Church.

Fort William, Calcutta

Madras was not a natural harbor, and for this and other reasons, the East India Company shifted its headquarters to Calcutta. Fort William, also designed on the star-shaped plan by a Captain Brohier, was situated next to a vast, open space that was created to allow it unrestricted field of fire. The civic buildings of the Company were built around this open space, known as the Maidan. This planning, in which the public buildings are outside the walls of the fort, is significant because it reflects the new sense of security the British enjoyed due to their increasing power and wealth.

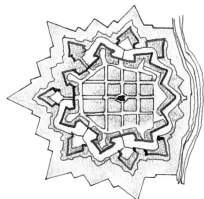

Above: Bengal was the center of the trading empire of the East India Company, and Fort William was the most important symbol of British military power in Asia. The bastions in this old photograph can be seen between St Peter's Church and the warren of barracks.

Left: Plan of Fort William. The original fort was largely destroyed by Siraj-ud-Daulah, the Nawab of Bengal, in 1756. Brohier's new design was completed in 1773.

Writers' Building, Calcutta

In 1780, the Writers' Building was constructed to house the junior clerks of the East India Company, making it the first civic building built by the British in India. Initially, this very long, plain building, said to be designed by a carpenter, Thomas Lyon, was like a barracks, strictly utilitarian and with very little architectural ornamentation. Its façade had repetitive but unremarkable windows and a balustraded parapet. The central part of the front façade was emphasised with Ionic pilasters. In 1880, the Writers' Building was given a major face-lift. Terracotta dressings with an ornate Corinthian façade and a dummy pedimented portico were added, so that it would fit in more with the notion of the Raj and its glory.

Commemorative Architecture

Lord Curzon's statue stands in front of an arch of the Calcutta Victoria Memorial (below), and is inscribed with the royal coat of arms.

As they firmly established themselves in India as a colonial power, the British commissioned statuary and structures to commemorate their sovereign and other luminaries of their empire. Memorials to the dead of imperial wars were also common. Architectural extravaganzas, these buildings celebrate milestones in the political and art history of India.

The Victoria Memorial, Calcutta

The Victoria Memorial has been called the most potent symbol of the British empire the world over. Commissioned by Lord Curzon in 1906 to rival the Taj in grandeur (which it never did), and to mark over 300 years of British presence in India and their growing might, it was a monument built in tribute to the Queen Empress. The building houses personal memorabilia relating to Queen Victoria's reign, and artefacts, documents and paintings that illustrate the progress of the British Indian empire. William Emerson was commissioned to carry out the work, which was supervised by Vincent Esch.

Lord Curzon specified that the building be designed either in the Classical or the Palladian style and also built of the same white Makrana marble as the Taj Mahal, to rival the beauty of the magnificent Mughal monument. A gigantic statue of Queen Victoria seated on a throne greets you long before you reach the entrance of the gleaming white museum.

The plan of the building consists of a large central part, flanked by two chambers separated from it by colonnaded corridors. The central chamber is roofed by a high dome and each corner of the building with smaller domes. Inside is a statue of Queen Victoria as a young girl. The dome is surmounted by a 5-meter-high bronze revolving statue of the Angel of Victory, symbolising British power.

The entire building is placed on a low marble plinth surrounded by reflecting pools and 26 hectares of gardens. The two open courts on each side also contain statues, one of them of Lord Curzon. The statuary was made in Italy and the building completed in 1921.

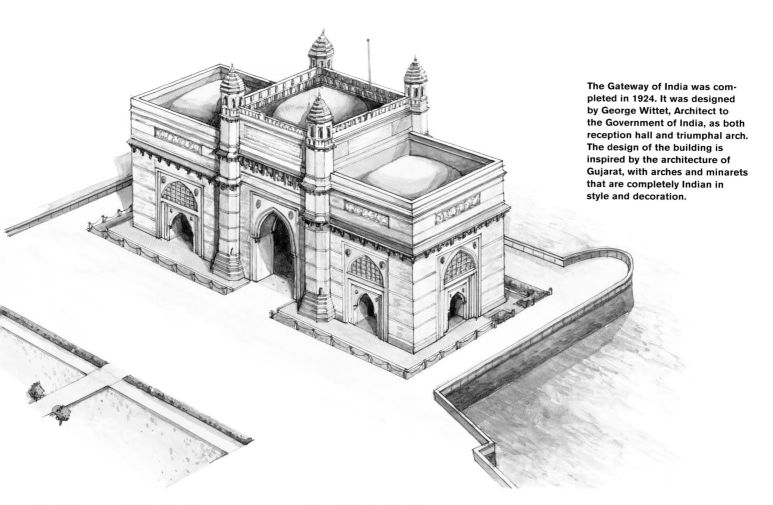

The Gateway of India was completed in 1924. It was designed by George Wittet, Architect to the Government of India, as both reception hall and triumphal arch. The design of the building is inspired by the architecture of Gujarat, with arches and minarets that are completely Indian in style and decoration.

The Gateway of India, Bombay

The Gateway of India was built as a triumphal arch under which George V and Queen Mary would pass when they disembarked at Bombay on their way to Delhi for the Coronation Durbar in 1911. Designed by George Wittet, it is built at the place where a 19th-century iron gazebo had earlier stood, welcoming newcomers across the seas to the empire in India. The side chambers of the triple-arched gateway were to serve as reception rooms. The semi-octagonal pilasters on either side of the main arch extend upwards and are capped with domed *chhattris*, joined together by a high parapet. Eaves supported on carved corbels accentuate the horizontal lines.

The Gateway of India is also remembered today because it marks the point from where the last battalion of the British Army departed on their journey back to England in 1947.

The All India War Memorial Arch, Delhi

Also called India Gate, the All India War Memorial Arch was completed in 1931. It was built after World War I as a memorial to Indian soldiers who died for the imperial cause in this and, along with the British, in the Afghan War of 1919. Designed by Sir Edwin Lutyens, the arch stands symbolically along the focal ceremonial driveway, Raj Path, facing a sandstone canopy, once housing the statue of King George V. The Arch is a colossal, honey-colored structure, 43 meters high, with delicately sculptured panels of stonework relief. The erection of the arch was as much a symbol of the British Raj as homage to India, and commemorates the ties which now bind the two countries. Since 1971, an eternal flame burns within the arch, in memory of the unknown Indian soldiers who lost their lives in the 1971 war against Pakistan.

The All India War Memorial Arch, popularly known as India Gate, is inscribed all over with names of the war dead.

Civic Buildings

Above and below: The Victoria Terminus, with rich ornamentation and a dome crowned by Thomas Earp's Statue of Progress.

Colonial architecture in India is largely remembered through the civic buildings that were designed by the British, not only because they were a part of the everyday lives of the people, but also because, as they evolved, the process of their design reflected the synthesis of the two architectural cultures. Early examples of civic architecture, which include town halls, railway terminuses, museums, law courts, municipal buildings, university buildings and libraries, were based entirely on design philosophies of the West, and the views of Indian associates were never invited. However, many of the architects and engineers were avowedly and unashamedly Orientalist in their leaning, and they spent long years studying and understanding the building traditions of the subcontinent. These men were responsible for the creation of an entirely new style that incorporated the local idiom, even if somewhat disdainfully, to create what came to be known as the definitive colonial architecture.

Victoria Terminus, Bombay

Bombay, the Victorian metropolis, was inspired above all by the Gothic revival in England, and the Victoria Terminus, labeled the finest Gothic building in India, is an architectural ode to the railways which, along with the postal system, were introduced to India by the British. The building was designed by Frederick William Stevens. Started in 1878, it took nine years to be completed. Modeled on St Pancras Station in London, the Victoria Terminus is a symmetrical building that combines Gothic elements such as pointed arches, vaults, dome and ornament. A massive masonry dome in the center provides the focus of the building, atop which stands the Statue of Progress. The ornamentation of the dome, as well as of the rest of the building, was the work of the Bombay Art School. Beneath the dome is a majestic staircase that opens onto landings on each of the three floors. The booking office is transverse to the axis, and has a

cross-vaulted ceiling painted blue with gold stars. Arches pierce the façades, emphasised by polychromatic stone and glazed tiles. The windows are filled with stained glass or delicate wrought-iron grillwork tracery. Turrets rise above the two tranverse projections on either side, their soaring verticality balancing the horizontal proportions of the building.

The ornamentation consists of floral designs and grotesque animals. The massive piers of the entrance gate support the British lion and the Indian tiger, probably the only asymmetrical elements in a building that is otherwise totally symmetrical.

Municipal Corporation Building, Bombay

Also designed by Stevens after he had left the Public Works Department and set up his own practice, the Bombay Municipal Corporation building was finished in 1893. It combines, surprisingly for Bombay, a city that favored an unadulterated Gothic aesthetic, the Indo-Islamic (or Indo-Saracenic) style with the Gothic in form and ornament. The vast staircase tower that rises in the center of the building proclaims its British origins, but the windows are framed by the cusped arch in the Indo-Islamic style, and the corner towers have bulbous domes of the same origin. A prominent masonry gable over the central entrance has a winged figure on it that represents the status of Bombay as the main metropolis in India.

University Convocation Hall and Library, Rajabai Tower, Bombay

Sir George Gilbert Scott, an eminent English architect, designed the University Convocation Hall and Library in Bombay, though he never visited India. The Convocation Hall, on one side of an oblong quadrangle, is designed and decorated in the early French style of the 15th century. The south end is apsidal and separated from the main body of the hall by a grand arch. A handsome carved timber gallery passes around three sides of the hall, supported on elegant cast-iron brackets. Light enters the interior through a stained-glass window. Externally, the most distinctive features are the open spiral staircases reminiscent of medieval French staircases.

The Library, on the other side, has arcaded galleries modeled on Venetian architecture, and is crowned by a pierced parapet of finely detailed stonework. Each corner of the building has open staircases, like the ones in the Convocation Hall, rising to the height of the building and surmounted by stone spires.

An immense tower was later added to the ensemble by an eminent Indian banker, Premchand Roychand, who provided the funds for the Rajabai Tower, in memory of his mother. It was based on the concept of the Italian *campanile* or bell tower, and is probably the most remarkable feature of the whole complex. The octagonal corona is surrounded by 2.5-meter-high sculptured figures representing the various castes of western India.

The Municipal Corporation Building, Bombay. The winged figure crowning the gable says "Urbs Prima in Indis."

Colonial Bungalows

Section of a typical bungalow, showing the central wide colonnaded verandah covered by a pitched roof and flanked on either side by Venetian windows. The more, or less, ornamental elements of the bungalow reflected the social status of the owner.

The term "bungalow" is conceptually and etymologically derived from *bangla*, the vernacular thatched roof hut of Bengal. The original *bangla* was a rectangular abode on a raised plinth, with the sloping roof projecting out to form a verandah supported on wooden pillars. The word was corrupted to bungalow and came to mean any single-storied house with a verandah.

The arrival of the Europeans in India, especially civilians, who were part of the great civic machinery of the Raj, gave rise to the need to provide homes that were more comfortable than the tents used by the military personnel. These homes not only had to be suited to the local climate, built from local materials and by local masons and carpenters, but also had to maintain the concepts of European identity and superiority. Social distancing from the "natives" was essential, and the bungalow was designed to facilitate this by various means: the large compound, enclosed by walls, gates and a watchman; the long driveway; the deep verandah; and even the insulating thick walls and high ceilings. The bungalow evolved as a response to these requirements and soon came to represent the ideal tropical colonial house, and was adopted as a prototype throughout the British empire.

From basically modest structures, bungalows soon developed into luxurious mansions, their size and form representing the social status of the occupants. The wooden posts, originally used to support the verandah, gave way to Doric and Tuscan columns. Elaborate carriage porches projected out to mark the entrance. Tiles replaced the earlier thatch, and ornamental balustrades were added. The English passion for gardens was translated into the bungalow being set amidst several hectares of land which were laid out on landscaping principles from back home. Classical detailing was superimposed on indigenous structures, not only to maintain the European identity but also to copy the grand town residences of Calcutta. Bungalows began to reflect, in their detailing, the architectural fashions of public buildings.

The Plan

The plan of the bungalow was basically rectangular, with a projecting colonnaded portico that led to a verandah on a high plinth, accessed from the portico by shallow steps. The verandah ran the entire length of the house, and was

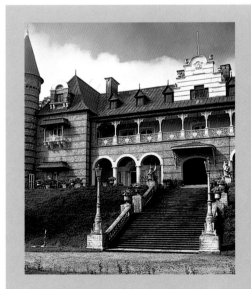

Chapslee Hall, Simla.

Hill Stations

The concept of the hill station was a result of the overwhelming need felt by the British to escape from the burning summer heat of the plains. Between 1815 and 1947, the British created over 80 hill stations or small towns nestling amongst the mountains of India. Three common features—sylvan, idyllic settings, an informal layout and a strict social hierarchy—distinguish every hill station in India.

The architecture of the colonial house in the hills was based more on vernacular housing traditions than on the colonial bungalow. These houses were constructed from local stone, quarried into squares, which were laid in courses with mortar to make thick walls. Every meter or so, the course was broken by a flat timber tie beam laid horizontally. Roofs were slated or shingled, over a shallow pitched form. Fretwork barge boards became a distinctive feature as did the wooden tie beams, which were left exposed to show the timber framing.

Many bungalows displayed a large variety of motifs and styles: fluted Doric, plain Tuscan, Venetian windows and Regency Gothic *quatrefoils*. Common devices were used to control temperature and light: Venetian shutters for the doors and windows, cane tatties suspended from verandahs, and latticework screens simulating the elaborately carved screens found in Mughal buildings.

usually open at its extreme ends as well. The centrally placed drawing room, the largest room in the house, opened off directly from the verandah and was connected to the dining room behind through an open archway. The dining room opened out on to a rear verandah, also deep and colonnaded, which overlooked the back garden. The drawing and dining rooms led off on either side to the other rooms. Windows and doors were arched, in the neoclassical style, with accentuated *voussoirs*. The kitchen was generally located in a separate outer building. The extensive grounds included modest quarters for the retinue of native servants required to maintain the bungalow.

Cooling Devices

The bungalow incorporated many devices, apart from thick walls, high ceilings and a deep verandah, to keep it cool. Doors and windows had Venetian louvered shutters and latticework screens to shut out the summer sun while letting in air. Ventilators, or small horizontally pivoted windows, were placed on walls near the ceiling to allow hot air to escape. In the summer months, the openings—doors and windows—were covered on the outside with finely woven reed screens called *chiks*, reminiscent of stone *jaalis*, which could be raised and lowered.

Sheets of muslin stretched across the room screened the pitched roof within while allowing air circulation. These sheets also kept lizards, snakes, rats and insects from entering the space below. In the summer, they were soaked with water. Curtains of *khus*, a scented reed, were also hung in front of openings and kept wet to cool the air that flowed inside. The ceilings often had hooks from which huge pieces of canvas or cloth were suspended on bamboo poles and attached to ropes so that they could be fanned across the room. These were the first *punkahs* or fans, and a small boy or *punkah-wallah* was specially employed to work the device.

Bungalows in the South

Bungalows in the south of the country, especially in Bangalore and Mysore, developed their own architectural style. Wide porch roofs and gables were enriched by elaborately carved barge boards and fretwork canopies known as "monkey tops." These were expressed as projecting pointed hoods over doors, windows and canopies enclosing verandahs and porches. In most Bangalore bungalows, roofs of verandahs were carried on huge teak beams, with the best of teak being imported from Burma. While most bungalows were single-storied, the Bangalore bungalow evolved into a two-storied home.

Indo-Colonial Architecture

The creation of the Indo-Colonial style—though frowned upon by purists as a hybrid, and by those who believed that British supremacy over India was best expressed by maintaining a distance from the natives—was an architectural expression of the complex relationship of give-and-take between the ruler and the ruled, the conqueror and the conquered.

The Laxmi Vilas Palace, Baroda, was known to be one of the most expensive buildings erected by a private individual, the Maharaja of Baroda, in the 19th century. Chisholm retained Charles Mant's original façade except for remodeling the design of the tower.

In his design of Mayo College, Ajmer, Charles Mant incorporated the "ancient indigenous style" instead of following the Classical or Gothic styles that were in fashion at the time. Yet he produced a building that was both suitable and modern, which he termed Indo-Saracenic.

The magic of the subcontinent was felt by many who came to India with the initial zeal of conquest, but soon discovered the complexity and wisdom that underscore the cultural traditions of India. To them goes the credit of recording, through meticulously prepared drawings, what had always been a subconscious pool of collective knowledge about the art of building. Their admiration for Indian architectural tradition, with its infinite ability to absorb and yet be distinctive, resulted in the creation of a language that would be acceptable to both traditions and cultures. The mix was often fanciful and self-conscious, not always successful, yet resulted in a grand effect befitting the Jewel of the East.

The Laxmi Vilas Palace, Baroda

This colossal palace was designed by Major Charles Mant, who then became obsessed that the structure might collapse (Mant also designed the Mayo College in Ajmer). It was completed twelve years later by Robert Fellowes Chisholm in 1890, after the death of Mant. The craftsmanship and materials used display a blend of "native" details with the needs of a modern palace. In plan it follows the traditional sections of public spaces and separate living quarters for the maharaja and the *zenana*. The Indo-Saracenic architectural style contains Hindu, Mughal, Jain and Gothic elements.

The Prince of Wales Museum, Bombay

The British excelled in museum design. The foundation stone of this museum was laid in 1905 by the Prince of Wales (future George V). It was modeled on the Gol Gumbaz of Bijapur (see p. 70), and designed by George Wittet (see p. 113). A scholarly interpretation of local Indian architecture of the 15th and 16th

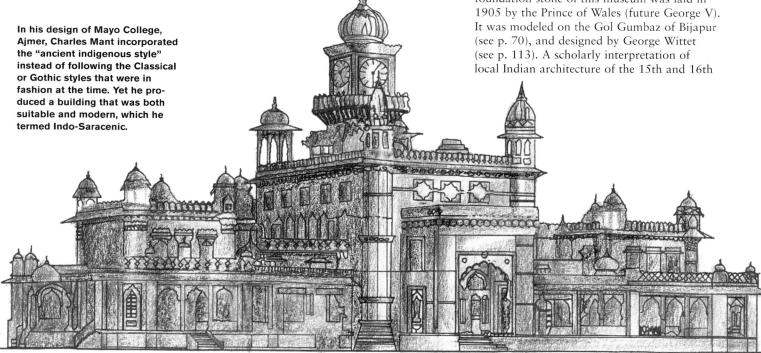

centuries, the museum was built of blue basalt and yellow sandstone. It has an immense concrete dome in the center with domelets all around, set in a garden lined with palm trees.

The National Art Gallery, Madras
Designed by Henry Irwin, the National Art Gallery in Madras is modeled on the Buland Darwaza of Fatehpur Sikri (see p. 118). Made of pink sandstone, the gallery is more Indian in architectural style than colonial.

The Gola, Patna
The Gola or Gol Ghar, meaning the Round House, was designed in 1786 by John Garstein. The Gola was a granary, with a storage capacity sufficient to provide food to the entire local population in days of famine. Based on the design of smaller, vernacular storehouses, this immense structure had symmetrical spiral ramps that led to the opening at the top from which the grain was poured into the dome's pit. A door on either side of one axis allowed the grain to be taken out, and cantilevered stone platforms along the side of the ramp provided resting places for sacks of grain.

Left: The National Art Gallery, Madras, formerly the Victoria Memorial Hall and Technical Institute, was built in 1909. An architectural gem, it is almost as good as the Mughal prototypes on which it is based.

Below: The Gola or Gol Ghar, Patna. The symbolic beehive form is dictated by its function as a granary. It tapers up to a height of over 27 meters, has a diameter of 33 meters, and walls 4 meters thick. The Gola is a symbol of the monumentalism aspired to by British architects.

Indian Patrons, Imperial Architects
Historical events resulted in many Indian princes accepting the sovereignty of the British empire, in return for which they were accorded respect, assured peace and allowed to indulge in their wildest fantasies, embodied perhaps in the building of extravagant palaces. Breaking away from traditional architecture, Indian rajas and princes proceeded to engage the leading British architects of the Raj to build extravaganzas that are a testimony to the political relationships between the old and new rulers of India. These palaces were at best a harmonious synthesis between existing and imported traditions, and at worst, a florid and inelegant juxtaposition of the two. The outstanding example of these palaces include the Amba Vilas Palace at Mysore (right), designed by Henry Irwin, the Lalgarh Palace at Bikaner, designed by Sir Samuel Swinton Jacob, and the Laxmi Vilas Palace at Baroda (opposite above).

Lutyens' Delhi

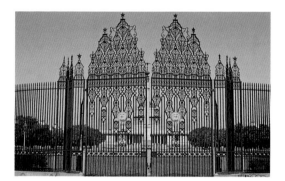

A memorial bust of Edwin Landseer Lutyens made by HAN Medd, seen on the grand open staircase at Rashtrapati Bhawan.

Right: The ornamental iron gate to Rashtrapati Bhawan was copied by Lutyens from a pair he saw in Chiswick, England.

Below: Larger than Versailles, Rashtrapati Bhawan's north and south blocks rise from the surrounding plain, while the east and west fronts are built on an elevated platform.

Built atop the mound of Raisina Hill, the Viceroy's House was the focal point of the new capital city of New Delhi, the last of Delhi's seven cities to be built over centuries. Both city and palace were designed by the British architect Sir Edwin Lutyens to represent the might, power and strength of the imperial British empire, a politically fitting tribute to India, the jewel in the British crown.

Lutyens himself had never visited India but his wife was the daughter of a former Viceroy, and a follower of the Theosophists, who had their base at Madras. She was strongly in favor of Indian independence, a movement that was beginning to dilute more uncompromising values of imperialism. Though the British continued to regard themselves as wholly superior, they realised that they had much to learn from the "uncivilised" natives. The winds of Modernism were also beginning to blow across the West, and Lutyens was undoubtedly affected by these events. Though Lutyens disliked traditional Indian architecture and resisted appointing Indian elements to Western shapes, his architectural interpretation of the qualities of British imperialism was to create a blend that eschewed the florid and the ostentatious, and relied on proportion, selective ornamentation, the understanding of local materials and their natural colors, and the role of sciography. In form and manner, the building is clearly classical, but outwardly recognised by obvious elements from both Buddhist and Mughal architecture.

Commissioned to build New Delhi in 1911, Lutyens considered the element of timelessness as essential an ingredient of the monumental as grandeur of scale. The Viceroy's House, now the residence of the President of India and renamed the Rashtrapati Bhawan, along with

136

the spectacular Mughal Gardens that adjoin it, are testimony to the fact that he achieved this.

A massive dome dominates the outline of the building. The shape of the dome, which is simultaneously classical as well as Buddhist in origin, makes a strong statement of the synthesis of two cultures, which is followed through in the other elements. A 2.5-meter-deep Mughal *chhajja* covers the colonnade, and *chhattris* emphasise the skyline. Lutyens' knowledge of both sciography as well as color and texture are evident in the manner in which red sandstone has been used to break the lines and create a contrast to the cream-colored Dholpur stone, which has been used to construct the building.

The H-shaped sprawling building covers 1.8 hectares of land. As you enter through the ornate wrought-iron gates, interspersed with carved sandstone piers, the ceremonial aspect is emphasised by an honorific column surmounted by a lotus and star, and the immense court of crushed red sandstone where state visitors are received. You continue up a wide flight of stairs and through a huge door into the Durbar Hall.

The circular 24-meter-high Durbar Hall, set under the dome, pierced with a central skylight, dominates the principal floor of the interior. Originally the throne room, this space is now used for important state occasions.

Traditional Indian architectural vocabulary, from Mauryan to Mughal, is blended with that of the classical West. Each wing has a different function. The east is used for state occasions, the south is for domestic use, the north houses the vast administrative machinery, while the west is reserved for recreation.

Brilliantly suited to its original purpose as a Viceregal Palace, the Rashtrapati Bhawan is one of the triumphs of 20th-century architecture and a masterpiece of the unique Anglo-Indian Imperial style.

The central dome (left) and section of the Rashtrapati Bhawan (below).

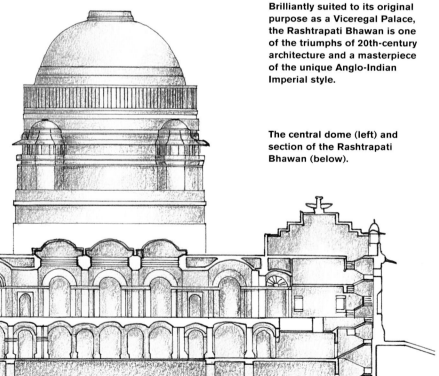

Modern Architecture and Le Corbusier

The year 1947 saw the freedom of India from British rule, and the traumatic partition of the subcontinent into two nations—India and Pakistan. Despite the wounds caused by the division of the country, Jawaharlal Nehru, the first Prime Minister, articulated the dreams of the Indian people at large when he spoke of a new India, free of the shackles of colonial rule, which would "awaken to new life and freedom."

Le Corbusier's paintings on one of the entrance doors of the Assembly Hall.

With the partition of India, the gracious capital of the state of Punjab, Lahore, became a part of Pakistan. Indian Punjab needed a new capital that would be, in Nehru's words, "the temple of a new India ... unfettered by the traditions of the past." Nehru invited Le Corbusier, the renowned Swiss architect, to design this new city. Corbusier was an advocate of the architectural philosophy of Modernism, derived from the principles of the Bauhaus School. The site of the new city, Chandigarh—abode of the goddess Chandi—was on a vast plateau along the foothills of the Himalayas.

Le Corbusier, like Lutyens, eschewed, and was extremely antagonistic to, superficial embellishment, which is how he perceived the decorative lexicon of traditional Indian architecture. Unlike Lutyens, however, who despite his distaste nevertheless used established Indian

architectural features as symbols, Corbusier respected the value of certain basic elements as essential to counter the primary parameter of India's harsh climate. Although the buildings that he created have no commonality with the imagery of architecture that had developed in the subcontinent over the previous 3,000 years, they are celebrated as a landmark in the evolution of not only Indian but international architectural thought and expression.

Like the Colonial style, Corbusier's work created another break from the slow amalgamation, synthesis and evolution of styles that had been the hallmark of the earlier architectural traditions. An entire generation of young architects, mostly with an Anglicised background and education, began to espouse Corbusier's philosophy of form, material and structural expression, and used these as a basis

The Secretariat, one of the three principal buildings of the Capitol Complex, Chandgarh. It displays all the devices Corbusier employed to counter the harshness of the North Indian climate: the overhanging horizontal roof, recessed windows or *brise-soleil*, and open spaces interspersed between pillars, which allowed the building to "breathe."

for their architecture. This was reinforced by the effects of a worldwide boom in technological advancement which allowed architects to be exposed to and explore new materials such as concrete and steel, whose plasticity and structural strength had not been experienced before. The architectural tenets of internationalism were thus no longer confined to the industrialised nations of the West.

The master plan of Chandigarh was a realisation of 30 years of earlier research and theorising by Le Corbusier. The formula developed by him was based on a hierarchical grid system. Heading it was the Capitol Complex, the architectural showpiece of Chandigarh. The fundamentals of his design inventory can be read in all three major buildings here: the Secretariat, the Assembly Hall and the High Court. The first invention was the *brise-soleil*, a sun-breaking device, where recessed windows were set in a projecting crate-like framework that gave a rich texture of light and shade to the building. The second was the horizontal roof extending well over the walls of the building (*parasol*). This was supported on pillars with open spaces in between (*pilotis*) to allow the free flow of air. With these he transformed the traditional decorative windows, verandahs, pavilions and halls into a dramatically new modern idiom.

Le Corbusier was also invited to the textile city of Ahmedabad by a leading industrialist family, the Sarabhais, to design both public and private buildings. Here too, Indian imagery offered him a valuable resource to translate into his own vocabulary for India, visible in the Millowners' Association, a sort of club for the industrialist élite, a museum and two houses.

Architecture in India Today

Today, more than forty years after Corbusier's Chandigarh, Indian architects are struggling between the pressures of modernity and the values of tradition. Modern Indian architecture is faced with a bewildering plurality of choice—between a globalised, modern, industrial sensibility on the one hand, and locale, and culture-specific, craft-based traditions on the other.

Charles Correa's Jawahar Kala Kendra in Jaipur. Correa emphasises the importance of building with Indian living patterns in mind and stresses the need for a number of interconnected units.

Balkrishna Doshi's own office and research center at Sangath, Ahmedabad, uses earth forms, open terraces and water channels to create an environment that is suitable to both the local climate and ethos.

The Early Modernists

Chandigarh opened up a new era of architecture in India. Concrete, as the new building material, acquired its own visually powerful aesthetic. After Independence, young Indian architects had already begun to go abroad to study. They brought back with them the new ideas that were sweeping across the West and found India receptive to them. A. P. Kanvinde had studied under Walter Gropius in Boston, Balkrishna Doshi had worked with Le Corbusier in his atelier in Paris, Habib Rahman, Charles Correa and a host of others were also influenced by the American Modern Movement.

Corbusier fired the creativity of the profession in Chandigarh and Ahmedabad; American architect Louis Kahn revived the aesthetic of brick in his Indian Institute of Management at Ahmedabad. The first truly modern building to be designed in India is seen by many, however,

as the Aurobindo Ashram, Golconde, at Pondicherry, the work of a Czech architect, Raymond Antonin (1948). Golconde exemplifies the principles of a modern architecture relevant to the Indian context: parallel horizontal louvers cut by thin concrete vaulting in a crate-like system provide cross ventilation and sun protection. The work is true to Antonin's beliefs and the spirit of Modernism—"structurally clean and pure ... simple, direct and most economical."

Earlier decades of independent India brought with them not only the enormous challenges of building and planning a new urban India, but the promise of large commissions in public and institutional building. Many of the outstanding earlier works therefore remain modern Indian architecture's landmarks, placing their authors in an unrivalled position at the top of the architectural pyramid.

Kanvinde designed several institutions, universities, and industrial and housing complexes of which his Indian Institute of Technology at Kanpur combined the requirements of expansion, pedestrian and vehicular movement and landscape in a masterly manner that works efficiently till today. Charles Correa's seminal Gandhi Smarak Sangrahalaya (memorial to Mahatma Gandhi) in Ahmedabad reflects his ongoing concern for simplicity of form and material, concern for climate, and concepts that capture the essence of the requirement. Correa, also an author, has also been a think-tank for many of the government's forum on urban issues. Balkrishna Doshi's best works are based in Ahmedabad, where he lives, and include Sangath (1980), his own office and research center, and the exposed brick Indian Institute of Management at Bangalore. Raj Rewal established himself with the Permanent Exhibition complex (1972) and the Asiad Village (1982), both at Delhi. A host of others form part of the modern architecture family, combining with

their creative talents the skills of teaching and writing. Among foreign architects who settled down in India and made their mark are Joseph Allen Stein in Delhi and Laurie Baker in Kerala. Fariburz Sahba, an Iranian architect, designed the lotus-shaped Baha'i Temple, a structural and conceptual masterpiece in white marble.

Younger generations continue to be bewildered by the choices in material and the demands of a swiftly evolving globalised society.

The International Style

In the early post-Independence years, the heterogeneous architectural identity of India was juxtaposed with a homogeneous uniformity of expression that was one of the products of Modernism. Efficiency, functionality, economic viability, regularity as opposed to symmetry and dependence on the instrinsic quality of materials instead of applied decoration, were the tenets of the modernist sensibility and they were often perceived to be in conflict with tradition. The International style was the aesthetic and technological response to the modernist movement and was based on a new economic world order without climatic, geographical and cultural barriers, and with a global identity.

The Revival of Traditions

The opening of the economy in 1991 positioned India at the edge of a new building boom, bringing with it the promise of new opportunities for architects to showcase their talents. Many architects in India today feel that Indian architecture needs to express this global identity and that, to achieve its expression, the burden of traditionalism has to be shed. Thus, concrete, steel and glass towers, commissioned by a small élite group with a "modern" sensibility, express one trend in contemporary urban architecture.

The last few decades have made it evident, however, that the solutions to many of India's architectural needs, especially that of providing housing for the majority of the citizens of the world's second most populated country, do not lie in modernist responses. This is especially true of rural India, where most of the country's people live, and where many basic needs like sustainable livelihoods, educational and health facilities, drinking water and electricity are still unattainable. Many architects have realised the disastrous consequences of the import of an alien architectural philosophy, which relies on the use of energy-intensive materials and on an industrial sensibility of form, into a vastly

The Indian skyline is rapidly changing to accommodate the escalating rate of urbanisation.

In Thiruvananthapuram, Laurie Baker uses exposed brick in innovative ways as in the Center for Development Studies.

Designed by Raj Rewal, architect of many landmark buildings in New Delhi, the Parliament Library occupies a prized location, with Rashtrapati Bhawan, the Secretariat buildings and Parliament House as its neighbors. The complex of horizontally spaced groups of low-lying domes resonates with its surroundings. Lightweight fiber cement, steel lattice and tensile cables and glass bricks filter light to the spaces below. Inspired by historic architectural models, this contemporary building is designed to evoke the spirit of enlightenment and democracy.

different environment—climatically, ecologically, culturally and economically. The need to find solutions in traditional wisdom and knowledge systems that had proved their practical as well as spiritual and emotional viability has led to the revival of age-old traditions in the fields of arts, crafts and building methodologies. The work of architects of this discipline reflects an attempt to understand the holistic nature of urban and architectural planning and expression, and its traditional underpinnings. The connection between spaces and climate, materials, social customs, ecology, economics and spirituality cannot be ignored.

Postmodernism in India

The loss of identity that was one of the results of Modernism has led to yet another trend, where many architects seek an aesthetic solution in the forms and architectural identities of the past, while still adhering to the basic principles of the International style. The process of assimilation that was an integral part of India's architectural heritage has found new expression in the revival and quest for these identities. The Postmodernist response of "less is a bore" to

Modernism's motto of "less is more," layered with a remarkable range of traditions to choose from, has resulted in an eclectic and sometimes injudicious amalgamation of these elements. It is not an uncommon sight to see buildings, especially in cities, where Doric columns abut Mughal *jaalis*, and where traditional carved railings reminiscent of the *havelis* of Jaisalmer are mounted on parapets of houses whose walls are punctured with triangles and circles in the Modernist style.

The Indian love of the ornate is also reflected in Postmodernist interiors—even small fast food restaurants boast elaborate ceilings with gilt and plaster-of-paris patterns of classical origins, and walls of ceramic tiles with images of Hindu gods. The use of modern industrial technologies and materials to recreate forms that were essentially the product of a different craft sensibility is a contradiction apparent in the kitsch of Postmodern Indian architecture.

Contemporary architecture in India thus reflects the bewildering choices provided by a rich architectural heritage as well as both the necessity and difficulty in finding solutions to the larger problems faced by the country.

Glossary

Adisthana plinth on which South Indian temple stands
Amalaka flat-ribbed, melon-shaped ornament
Anda hemispherical dome of the *stupa*
Antarala vestibule which leads to the *garbha griha* in the Nagara style
ardha mandapa porch that leads to the *mandapa* of a temple
Bagh garden
Baithak reception room or drawing room
Bangaldar curved roof derived from the shape of roofs in Bengali huts
Baoli stepwell
Baradari open pavilion with three attached openings on each side
Baramdah verandah
Bhog mandir see *nat mandir*
Bhool bhulaiya labyrinth of passageways
Burj tower with imposing superstructure
Cella Latin term for the sanctum of a temple
Chahar/Charbagh garden divided into four quadrants
Chaiti sacred place
Chaitya Buddhist hall of worship, with apsidal ending
Chattravali series of *chattris*
Chhajja sloping projection from façade
Chhattri kiosk or small pavilion on roof
Chorten votive structures to honor Buddhist saints
Darwaza doorway in Muslim architecture
Deul shrine and superstructure in Orissa temples
Dharamshalas rest houses
Diwan-i-Am Hall of Public Audience
Diwan-i-Khas Hall of Private Audience
Dukhang core of the temple in the Himalayan monastery
Durbar court or meeting hall
Durg fort
Dwara doorway
Ek ratna single-towered Bengal temple
Gandi curvilinear *shikhara* of the *deul*
Garbha griha *sanctum sanctorum*, most sacred part of the Hindu temple
Ghat riverbank or steps leading to water
Gompa Himalayan monastery

Gonkhang chamber for meditation and ritual in the Himalayan monastery
Gopuram monumental gateway to a South Indian temple
Gudha mandapa assembly hall
Gumbad dome
Harmika railing around the summit of the *stupa*
Haveli house built around a courtyard
Hujra vaulted chamber
Idgah praying place used during Muslim festivals
Imam Muslim priest
Imambara religious structure used for Shiite Muharram festival
Iwan roofed or vaulted hall opening onto a courtyard
Jaali Latticed screen, in stone or in wood
Jagamohan dance or assembly hall in Hindu temples of Orissa
Jami Masjid congregational mosque
Jawab identical building used for the sake of symmetry
Jhakhang temple within the Himalayan monastery
Jharokha window fully or partially closed
Kalasha vase-shaped urn found in filials
Kalyana mandapa hall for divine marriage ceremonies
Kankani freestanding gateway
Khwabgah sleeping chamber of an emperor
Kinathara raised platform used for prayer and seating in a Kerala Muslim house
Kirtistambha victory tower
Kolam decorative motifs created with rice powder or chalk
Kotla citadel
Kudu decorative motif symbolising the residence of the gods
Kund temple tank
Langar free kitchen in a Sikh *gurudwara*
Linga phallic emblem of the god Shiva
Liwan Islamic pillared cloisters with many entrances
Madrassa school for religious learning
Mandala symbolic diagram, consisting of circles and rectangles showing the world in its cosmic development

Mandapa temple hall for public rituals
Mashaka uppermost unit in the *shikhara*
Mihrab prayer niche, indicating the direction toward Mecca
Minar tower in a mosque from where the *muezzin* calls for prayer
Mimbar pulpit right of the *mihrab* on which the Koran is placed
Nat mandir hall for dance
Nav ratnas nine-towered Bengal temple
Pada base of a building temple
Pancha ratna five-towered Bengal temple
Pidha trapezoidal roof over the *jagmohan*
Pista plinth
Pradikshina patha circumambulatory path around a *stupa*
Qibla orientation toward Mecca
Qila fort
Qubba central domed chamber containing the *mihrab*
Rauza mausoloeum, funerary garden
Rekha deul Orissa temple tower
Sabha mandapa porch in Gujarat temples
Sehn rectangular courtyard with a tank in a mosque
Shikhara tower of a temple (North India)
Srikovil main shrine in a Kerala temple
Stambha column
Stupi rounded filial unit of a Dravidian temple
Tala story or level
Tarawad house of the Hindu Nair community of Kerala
Tehkhana basement
Tekkina place for domestic chores in a South Indian Nair house
Torana gateway to a *stupa*
Upapitha lower level of the *adisthana*
Vadakkina cooking area in a Hindu Nair house
Vaitul deul wagon-vaulted
Vav stepped well
Vedika fence/balustrade around a *stupa*
Veyaddi sacrificial altar of Vedic times
Vihara Buddhist monastery
Vimana tower of a temple (South India)
Ziarat pilgrimage tombs of saints
Zarih cenotaph
Zenana women's quarters

Bibliography

Alfieri, B. M., *Islamic Architecture of the Indian Subcontinent*, Ahmedabad: Mapin, 2000.

Archaeological Survey of India, *Archaeological Remains: Monuments and Museums*, Pts 1 and 2, Delhi, 1996.

Arshi, P. S, *Sikh Architecture in the Punjab*, New Delhi: Intellectual Publishing, 1986.

Aryan, K. C., *Basis of Decorative Element in Indian Art*, New Delhi: Rekha, 1988.

Bannerjee, G. N., *Hellenism in Ancient India*, Calcutta: Probstian, 1920.

Basham, A. L., *The Wonder That Was India*, London: Sedgwick and Jackson, 1954.

Batley, C., *The Design Development of Ancient Architecture*, London: Academy Editions, 1973.

Begley, W. E. and Desai, Z. A., *Taj Mahal: The Illumined Tomb*, Massachusetts: The Aga Khan Program for Islamic Architecture, 1989.

Brown, P., *Indian Architecture*, Vols 1 and 2, Bombay: Taraporewala, 1941 and 1956.

Bussagli, M., *Oriental Architecture*, New York: Abrams, 1973.

Davis, P., *Splendours of the Raj*, London: Penguin, 1987.

Deva, K., *Temples of North India*, New Delhi: National Book Trust, 1969.

Donaldson, T. E., *Hindu Temple Art of Orissa*, Vols 1–3, Leiden: E. J. Brill, 1987.

Doshi, S., *The Impulse to Adorn*, Bombay: Marg, 1982.

Grover, Satish, *The Architecture of India, Buddhist and Hindu*, 2nd edn, New Delhi: CBS Publishers and Distributors, 2003.

_____, *Islamic Architecture of India*, 2nd edn, New Delhi: CBS Publishers and Distributors, 2002.

Grunwadel, A., *Buddhist Art in India*, Varanasi: Bharatiya Publishing, 1974.

Harle, J. C., *The Art and Architecture of the Indian Subcontinent*, New York: Viking Penguin, 1986.

Havell, E. V., *The Ideals of Indian Art*, London: John Murray, 1911.

_____, *The Ancient and Mediaeval Architecture of India*, New Delhi: S. Chand, 1972.

_____, *Indian Architecture*, New Delhi: S. Chand, 1913.

Herdeg, K., *Formal Structure in Indian Architecture*, New York: Rizzoli, 1990.

Hoag, J., *Islamic Architecture*, New York: Abrams, 1977.

Huntington, S. L. and Huntington, J. C., *The Art of Ancient India: Buddhist, Hindu, Jain*, New York: Weatherhill, 1993.

Iman, Abu, *Sir Alexander Cunningham and the Beginning of Indian Archaeology*, Dhaka: Asiatic Society of Pakistan, 1966.

Irving, R. G., *Indian Summer*, New Haven: Yale University, 1982.

Koch, Ebba, *Mughal Architecture*, New Delhi: TBI, 1991.

Kramrisch, Stella, *The Art of India*, London: Phaidon, 1954.

_____, *Hindu Temples*, Vols 1 and 2, New Delhi: Motilal Banarsidas, 1946.

_____, *Indian Sculpture*, Calcutta: YMCA, 1933.

Meister, Michael W. and Dhaky, M. A. (eds.), *Encyclopedia of Indian Temple Architecture*, Vols 1–4, Philadelphia: University of Pennsylvania, 1983–91.

Metcalf, T. R., *An Imperial Vision*, London: Faber, 1968.

Michell, George, *Architecture of the Islamic World*, London: Thames and Hudson, 1995.

_____, *Brick Temples of Bengal*, Princeton: Princeton University Press, 1983.

_____, *Hindu Art and Architecture*, London: Thames and Hudson, 2000.

Morris, J., *Stones of Empire*, London: Penguin, 1984.

Mukerji A., *Ritual Art of India*, London: Thames and Hudson, 1985.

Pal, P., *Jain Art from India*, London: Thames and Hudson, 1995.

Pereira, J., *Elements of Indian Architecture*, New Delhi: Motilal Banarsidas, 1987.

_____, *Islamic Sacred Architecture*, New Delhi: Books and Books, 1994.

Rowland, Benjamin, *The Art and Architecture of India*, London: Penguin, 1953.

Sarkar, H., *Early Buddhist Architecture in India*, New Delhi: Munshiram Manoharlal, 1966.

Sivaramamurthy, C., *The Art of India*, New York: Abrams, 1977.

_____, *Early Indian Architecture*, Vols 1 and 2, New Delhi: Munshiram Manoharlal, 1991.

_____, *Panorama of Jain Art*, New Delhi: TOI, 1983.

Soundara Rajan, K. V., *Indian Temple Styles*, New Delhi: Munshiram Manoharlal, 1972.

Speaking Stones: World Cultural Heritage Sites in India, New Delhi: Eicher Goodearth, 2001.

Tadgell, Christopher, *The History of Indian Architecture: From the Dawn of Civilization to the End of the Raj*, London: Architecture, Design, and Technology Press, 1990.

Tillotson, G. H. R., *Paradigms of Indian Architecture: Space and Time in Representation and Design*, SOAS Collected Papers on South Asia, 13, London: Curzon Press, 1997.

_____, *Rajput Palaces*, New Haven: Yale University Press, 1987.

Varma, P., *Mansions at Dusk*, New Delhi: Spantech, 1992.

Volwahsen, A. and Stierlin, Henri (eds.), *Architecture of the World: India*, Cologne: Benedikt Taschen, 1993.

_____, *Architecture of the World: Islamic India*, Cologne: Benedikt Taschen, 1993.

Zimmer, Heinrich R., *The Art of Indian Asia*, Princeton: Princeton University Press, 1955.

_____, *Myths and Symbols in Indian Art and Civilization*, Princeton: Princeton University Press, 1972.